THE KREGEL PICTORIAL GUIDE TO THE NEW TESTAMENT

ROBERT W. YARBROUGH

CONTENTS

The New Testament: Witness to God's Faithfulness	2
Jesus' Life and Message	4
Matthew	6
Mark	8
Luke	10
John	12
Acts	14
Paul's Early Letters (Galatians; 1–2 Thessalonians)	16
Paul and Corinth (1–2 Corinthians)	18
Paul and Rome	20
Paul's Later Letters (Prison and Pastoral Epistles)	22
Hebrews	24
1 and 2 Peter	26
James, John, and Jude	28
Revelation	30
For Further Reading	32

The New Testament:
Witness to God's Faithfulness

The New Testament was written by personal disciples of Jesus or, in a few cases, their close associates. No other writings exist with such good claims to be authentic, first-century records of what Jesus and his earliest followers did and taught.

The New Testament therefore deserves our utmost attention and respect. It sets forth three ways in which Jesus Christ became both a servant of all and yet at the same time the Lord over all. Each of these ways is rooted in God's previous Old Testament promises.

The Cross
God promised Abraham that he would make a great nation of his descendents (Gen. 15:5); Jesus' very name signified that he would "save his people from their sins" (Matt. 1:21). "His people" were the believing children of Abraham of Old Testament times as well as those who became "children of Abraham" by faith in Christ in New Testament times (Gal. 3:7). The way Jesus saved us was by dying on the cross for our sins.

In the Old Testament era, God taught his people that their sin deserved punishment. It demanded, in fact, their death! But there could be forgiveness if people would heed God's word through his verbal guidance (*torah*, law or teaching) and prophets. Through response to what God said to them—"Hear, O Israel!" (Deut. 6:4)—they could express repentance and faith that would lead to God's blessing (life) rather than his displeasure (death). In Deuteronomy, Moses frequently presents these stark

A typical artist's impression of Jesus of Nazareth. But who was Jesus? What was he really like?

alternatives to the Hebrew people.

Yet the Old Testament laws and sacrifices pointed to something greater than themselves, just as Moses pointed to a prophet far greater than he was (Deut. 18:15; see Acts 3:22). The Old Testament points to a sin sacrifice offered by God himself (Isa. 53:6).

The New Testament identifies Jesus as the one who gave his life as ransom for many (Mark 10:45). He became sin in our place so that in him we might become God's righteousness (2 Cor. 5:21). As Moses lifted up the bronze snake, Jesus was lifted up so that those who believe in his death for their sins will "not perish but have eternal life" (John 3:14, 16).

The saving center of the New Testament is the message of Christ crucified for our sins.

The Resurrection
If Jesus had remained dead in the tomb, we would have no reason to believe that his death accomplished anything unusual. But following brutal death on a Roman cross, he was seen alive by many people on various occasions, ruling out theories that his appearances were hallucinations, personal visions, or some kind of hoax.

Old Testament Promises Fulfilled in Jesus Christ

Genesis 3:15	Satan crushed
Genesis 12:1–3	Blessing to all through Abraham
Exodus 12	Passover sacrifice
Deuteronomy 18:15	Prophet like Moses
2 Samuel 7:13	Eternal kingdom to son of David
Psalm 2	Futile rage against God's anointed one
Psalm 22	The suffering of Christ
Isaiah 2:2–5	The coming kingdom
Jeremiah 31:31–34	The new covenant
Malachi 4:5	The forerunner to Jesus Christ

A Rabbi from Bible times.

A tomb with a roll-away stone. The New Testament hinges on Jesus' resurrection.

Few facts of ancient history are more certain than that Jesus' disciples claimed to see him alive after his death.

Jesus said that his resurrection was foreshadowed by what the Old Testament taught. After the Christ suffered, he would be glorified (Luke 24:26). "Thus it is written," said Jesus, "that the Christ should suffer and on the third day rise from the dead" (v. 46 ESV). As Jonah was swallowed by the fish but was later given a new lease on life, so Jesus was claimed by death and the tomb but rose to send forth a saving message (see Matt. 12:40). As Abraham received Isaac back from what seemed like certain death (Heb. 11:19), Jesus was given back alive to his disciples following his death under Pontius Pilate.

Numerous Old Testament incidents point to a belief that God could and did raise the dead. Jesus vindicated that tenacious belief in an astonishing and history-changing way.

The Ascension

The Easter message, "Christ is risen, he is risen indeed," is a grand climax of the New Testament. But the story of Jesus does not end there. Rather, it moves to a new plane: he ascended into heaven. The same disciples who saw him alive following his crucifixion saw him "lifted up, and a cloud took him out of their sight" (Acts 1:9).

Jesus himself taught that somehow the mighty God of heaven had someone at his right hand whom David called "Lord" (Matt. 22:43–45). This was such a difficult concept that when Jesus brought it up, his interrogators simply dropped the subject (v. 46). And yet it was clearly affirmed in Psalm 110:1. This psalm is quoted or alluded to in the New Testament perhaps two dozen times.

Another memorable portrait from the Old Testament depicts God on his throne, "the Ancient of Days," presenting "dominion and glory and a kingdom" to someone called "a son of man" (Dan. 7:13–14). In the Gospels, "Son of Man" is Jesus' most frequent self-designation.

Not only, then, did Jesus rise from the dead to be witnessed by many, he returned to God's presence where he exercises dominion over all creation.

The New Testament's Message

"Believe in God, believe also in me," Jesus said (John 14:1). But what does believing in Jesus involve? The twenty-seven books of the New Testament go far toward answering that question.

Comparative Lengths of New Testament Books

Matthew
Mark
Luke
John
Acts
Romans
1 & 2 Corinthians
Galatians
Ephesians
Philippians
Colossians
1 & 2 Thessalonians
1 & 2 Timothy
Titus
Philemon
Hebrews
James
1 & 2 Peter
1, 2 & 3 John
Jude
Revelation

He was manifested in the flesh, vindicated in the Spirit, seen by angels, preached among the nations believed in the world, taken up in glory.
1 Timothy 3:16

Jesus' Life and Message

Details about Jesus' early years are sketchy. Yet they indicate two things. First, he was born to Jewish parents, had brothers and sisters, received the religious instruction provided by the synagogue, and learned the carpenter's trade. In other words, he appeared to be a normal first-century Jewish male of Galilee. Second, he was conceived without a human father, was hailed as a king at birth by angels and wise men, and confounded religious scholars when he was just a boy of twelve. In other words, he was clearly more than a normal Galilean tradesman. This tension between human normalcy, on the one hand, and a spiritual stature that was anything but normal, on the other, runs throughout his life.

Galilean Ministry

Some scholars put the beginning of Jesus' ministry around A.D. 27, others A.D. 30. In either case, Jesus' public ministry was about three years in length, since it spanned three annual Passover feasts (John 2:13; 6:4; 12:1). Jesus emerged into the public eye when he received baptism from his cousin John "the Baptizer" in the Jordan River. John viewed the Jewish nation as estranged from God, and he called his hearers to repent, for "the kingdom of heaven is at hand" (Matt. 3:2). God was about to render judgment on his chosen people. Jesus had nothing to repent of, because he was sinless, but he accepted baptism, thereby endorsing John's message and identifying with the people he came to save. At baptism, Jesus also received the Father's confirmation that he loved and fully supported Jesus in his mission (Mark 1:11).

Following baptism, Jesus underwent weeks of stern testing in the desert. There, he established his mastery over the Devil and his resolve to complete his Father's mission according to the Father's will.

After John's imprisonment, Jesus called disciples. They followed him and learned from

A quiet stretch of the River Jordan.

him as he preached and healed the sick "throughout all Galilee" (Matt. 4:23). Crowds flocked to hear him from all surrounding regions (v. 25). The Sermon on the Mount (chaps. 5–7) is a good example of Jesus' message during this period, which lasted the better part of two years. It was not just *what* Jesus taught that amazed people; it was the *authority* with which he made his pronouncements (7:28–29).

Ministry Beyond Galilee

While Jesus' ministry focused on his fellow Jews (Matt. 15:24), he did not limit his preaching strictly to Galilee. He touched the life of a Samaritan woman and her fellow villagers (John 4). He ventured northward toward Tyre and Sidon and liberated the daughter of a Canaanite woman from an oppressive, demonic spirit (Matt. 15:21–28). Peter, at Caesarea Philippi, identified Jesus as "the Christ, the Son of the living God" (16:16). Probably on Mount Hermon, far removed from Galilee, three disciples witnessed Jesus conversing with Moses and Elijah. On this stunning occasion, Jesus' face and clothing shone with divine light (Matt. 17:1–13).

Cave beneath the modern Chapel of the Annunciation, Nazareth.

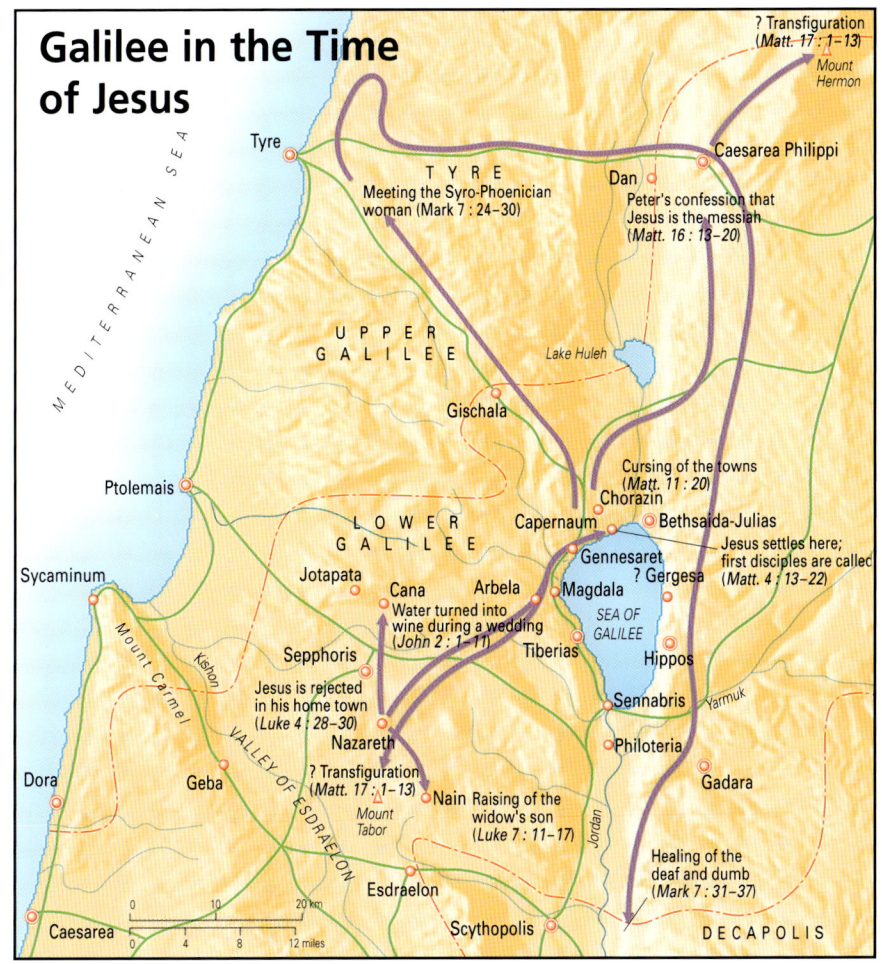

Galilee in the Time of Jesus

Star of Bethlehem

The best candidate for the famous "star of Bethlehem" described in Matthew 2 is a comet, recorded by Chinese astronomers, which appeared in the eastern sky in March, 5 B.C., and remained visible for about 70 days, moving slowly toward the south.

(Research by Prof. Colin Humphreys of Cambridge University: *Tyndale Bulletin* 43 [1992], 31–56)

By now Jesus was foretelling his crucifixion and resurrection, although his disciples did not understand.

Following some weeks outside Galilee, Jesus returned briefly to Capernaum. There, he reaffirmed many of his teachings, continued to heal and cast out demons, and again pointed to his coming death (vv. 22–23). The disciples were agitated by this. But as Jesus left Galilee and set his face toward Jerusalem for the last time (Luke 13:22; 17:11), there was little they could do but follow and expect the worst (John 11:16).

The Week the World Changed

The climactic event of Jesus' life was the Cross. It was then that he became what John the Baptist had called him three years earlier: "the Lamb of God who takes away the sin of the world" (John 1:29). Leading up to his crucifixion, Jesus raised Lazarus from the dead (chap. 11), entered Jerusalem to popular acclaim (12:12–19), continued to teach his disciples (chaps. 13–17), and instituted the meal of remembrance now called the Lord's Supper (Matt. 26:26–29).

Jesus lamented the opposition of Jerusalem's religious leaders to his message (Matt. 23:37–39). But in accordance with the Father's will, he surrendered himself to arrest and execution on charges of blasphemy and sedition. His death on the cross was in one sense a gross injustice, since he had committed no crime. Yet after burial he was exonerated—not by people, however, but by God. Jesus "was declared to be the Son of God in power . . . by his resurrection from the dead" (Rom. 1:4 ESV). The Resurrection showed God's acceptance of Jesus' sacrifice for human sin.

Jesus' Message

By Jesus' words and deeds he conveyed a twofold message.

First, *judgment and the need for righteousness*. All persons need to repent and seek a personal relationship with God. "Church" is not an institution but the community of those who share inner fellowship with God through faith in Christ and whose lives are centered on the furtherance of God's will. Eternal life is God's gift to those who seek him; eternal punishment awaits those who don't.

Second, *the saving face of God*. World religions abound in theories of the divine identity and the key to blessedness. In hindsight, Jesus' disciples could see that he is "the only God, who is at the Father's side." God the Father is invisible, but God the Son "has made him known" (John 1:18 ESV). Jesus taught he is the way, truth, and life (14:6). Those who put personal trust in him become recipients of the salvation that he made available through his death (3:16).

Matthew

The first gospel found in the New Testament is appropriately placed: it links back firmly to the Old Testament's history, writings, and message. Yet Matthew's message goes beyond its Old Testament foundation. What the Scriptures of Israel promised has now been fulfilled in the coming of Jesus of Nazareth.

Modern Study of the Gospels
A brief word is needed about how Matthew, and all the Gospels, should be regarded.

In the late eighteenth century the Gospels began to be read skeptically in centers of European learning. No longer were they viewed as divinely inspired and historically accurate. They were now seen as the product of solely human activity and social forces. The Gospels were no longer to be revered as the foundation of Christian confession; they were to be analyzed "critically." The Gospels were now viewed, at best, as sources of ethical direction or religious encouragement for modern humanity.

In this view, Mark eventually was seen to have been written first. Matthew and Luke, it was said, borrowed from Mark and added their own material, also drawing on a source that the critical analysts called "Q." It is supposed to have contained sayings of Jesus, although such a document has never been found. Many think it never existed. In the critical view, John made use of an independent body of information, or what scholars call "tradition." Thus for many scholars of the modern period, none of the Gospels came from eyewitnesses. None was written within a generation of Jesus' death. All the Gospels arose at least two generations after Jesus, and are the result of a process of literary borrowing, community creativity, and editorial shaping.

At its best, biblical scholarship is beneficial and valuable in many ways. But there is reason to be skeptical of "modern" skepticism of the four Gospels. Many scholars, in fact, remain convinced of the Gospels' historical reliability (see works by Blomberg in "For Further Reading"). In the following treatment of the four Gospels, the assumption is that they tell the truth about things Jesus did and said from his birth under Caesar Augustus until his death at the hands of Pilate in A.D. 30 or 33.

Matthew: From Tax Man to Teacher
Matthew, also called Levi (see Matt. 9:9; 10:3; Mark 2:14), was a tax collector. He worked for the Roman occupation forces, collecting money for his bosses and keeping a percentage for himself. This doesn't necessarily mean he was grossly dishonest. But it does mean he lived in the real world of money and political forces. He was not some naïve religious enthusiast living by spiritual imagination.

It is, therefore, all the more striking that hardheaded Matthew provides such a lofty portrait of Jesus. The closing verses of this gospel commission Jesus' followers to "make disciples of all nations . . . teaching them to do all" Jesus commanded them (Matt. 28:19–20). Through the gospel he

Palestine in the Time of Jesus

> As Jesus passed on from there, he saw a man called Matthew sitting at the tax booth, and he said to him, "Follow me." And he rose and followed him.
> Matthew 9:9 (ESV)

wrote, Matthew has now been doing so for nearly two millennia.

Who is the Jesus Matthew teaches?

The Jesus Matthew Knew

Matthew couldn't tell everything he remembered about Jesus. The scroll he worked on would only contain so much—about as much, it turns out, as is found in the twenty-eight chapters of "Matthew" in our New Testaments. But Matthew stressed several things. Together they form a core for understanding who Jesus was and what he called on all persons to do.

- *Jesus had no human father* (1:20). In a way we cannot explain, Mary became pregnant by God's direct act. Jesus was not less than human because of this. But he was more than a mere human. He inspired human awe even from the time of his conception.
- *Jesus fulfilled Old Testament prophecy* (see sidebar on page 2). Matthew sees eerie correlations between Jesus and the writings of the Old Testament, dating to hundreds of years earlier. About a dozen aspects of Jesus' life were foretold by prophets, among them Jesus' birth (1:23), his birthplace (2:6), Herod's murder of Jewish males when Jesus was born (2:18), Jesus' healing miracles (8:17), his use of parables (13:35), and the triumphal entry (21:5).
- *Jesus had a positive regard* for the Judaism of his time, yet, like John the Baptist, he called Israel to repent. "Repent" was central to John's message (3:2), and it was for Jesus' preaching too (4:17). The people of Judea and Galilee, and Jews all over the Roman world, needed to get right with God by acknowledging Jesus as their savior Messiah, or king.
- *Jesus had positive regard not only for other Jews but for Gentiles.* Jesus was Jewish and cared deeply for his ethnic kinsmen (23:37–39). But he cared deeply for all persons, even a Roman military officer (8:11–12). Non-Jews will enjoy heaven right alongside Abraham, Isaac, and Jacob.
- *Jesus is the Teacher without peer.* From the Sermon on the Mount (chaps. 5–7) to his last days on earth (28:18–20), Jesus lifted up his followers by his wise and piercing words. His words have equipped those who trust in him, "the church" (16:18; 18:17), to be messengers of Jesus' death and resurrection to all times and peoples ever since.

Outline of Matthew

1:1–17	Prologue: Jesus the bearer of Israel's promise
1:18–2:23	His birth, in fulfillmen of prophecy
3:1–9:35	Introducing the Son of God
3:1–4:25	Attested, tested, and into action
5:1–7:29	The authority of his word in his teaching
8:1–9:35	The authority of his word in his healing
9:36–12:50	Following the Son of God: issues of discipleship
13:1–16:12	The King, the Kingdom, and the rulers of Israel
16:13–20:34	Confessing the Son of God: issues of self-giving and suffering
21:1–23:39	The Son of God and the past: issues of Scripture, people, and interpretation
24:1–25:46	The Son of God and the future: issues of judgment and salvation
26:1–28:20	The Son of God, crucified, risen, and Lord of all

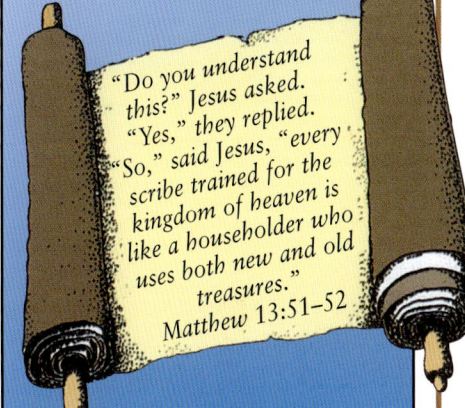

> "Do you understand this?" Jesus asked. "Yes," they replied. "So," said Jesus, "every scribe trained for the kingdom of heaven is like a householder who uses both new and old treasures."
> Matthew 13:51–52

The Church of the Holy Sepulchre, Jerusalem, probable site of Jesus' death and burial.

Mark

Author
For most of church history, Mark's gospel was viewed as a sort of condensation of the much longer Matthew and Luke. Since the mid-nineteenth century it has been viewed as the first gospel to be written. Regardless of its order of appearance, Mark tells about Jesus from a distinct point of view. Reports dating back to A.D. 100 or earlier associate this gospel with the apostle Peter. Mark is said to have been Peter's interpreter, his assistant as he preached. Near the time of Peter's death, Mark wrote down a selection of the Petrine presentation of Jesus.

We know several things about this Mark. He is the young man called "John" who left his Jerusalem home and accompanied Paul and Barnabas on their first missionary trip (Acts 13:5). But for unknown reasons he left to return home (Acts 13:13). Shortly thereafter he was at the center of a dispute between Paul and Barnabas (Acts 15:37–39). Mark and Paul were later reconciled (see Col. 4:10; Philem. 24; 2 Tim. 4:11). Mark's association with Peter in Rome, perhaps a dozen years later, is hinted at in 1 Peter 5:13.

Purpose
Some argue that Mark wrote to encourage the Roman church around the time of the Neronian persecution (A.D. 60s). Others observe that Mark presents Jesus as both Son of God and the servant Son of Man (10:45); they suggest this may be viewed as his purpose in writing. It is possible that Mark just wanted to preserve a selection of Peter's reminiscences, whose value for the church after his death would be self-evident.

Distinctive Features
Unlike Matthew, Mark highlights Jesus' actions more than his teachings. The word "immediately" occurs over forty times. In rapid-fire fashion, Mark moves the reader from one incident in Jesus' life to another.

Mark lays stress on the emotions of Jesus. We see him moved by feelings like compassion (1:41; 6:34; 8:2), indignation (3:5; 8:12; 10:14), and distress and sorrow (14:33–34). Twice we are told that he sighed (7:34; 8:12), perhaps expressing impatience or wistfulness. Jesus, then, knew the ups and downs of human existence.

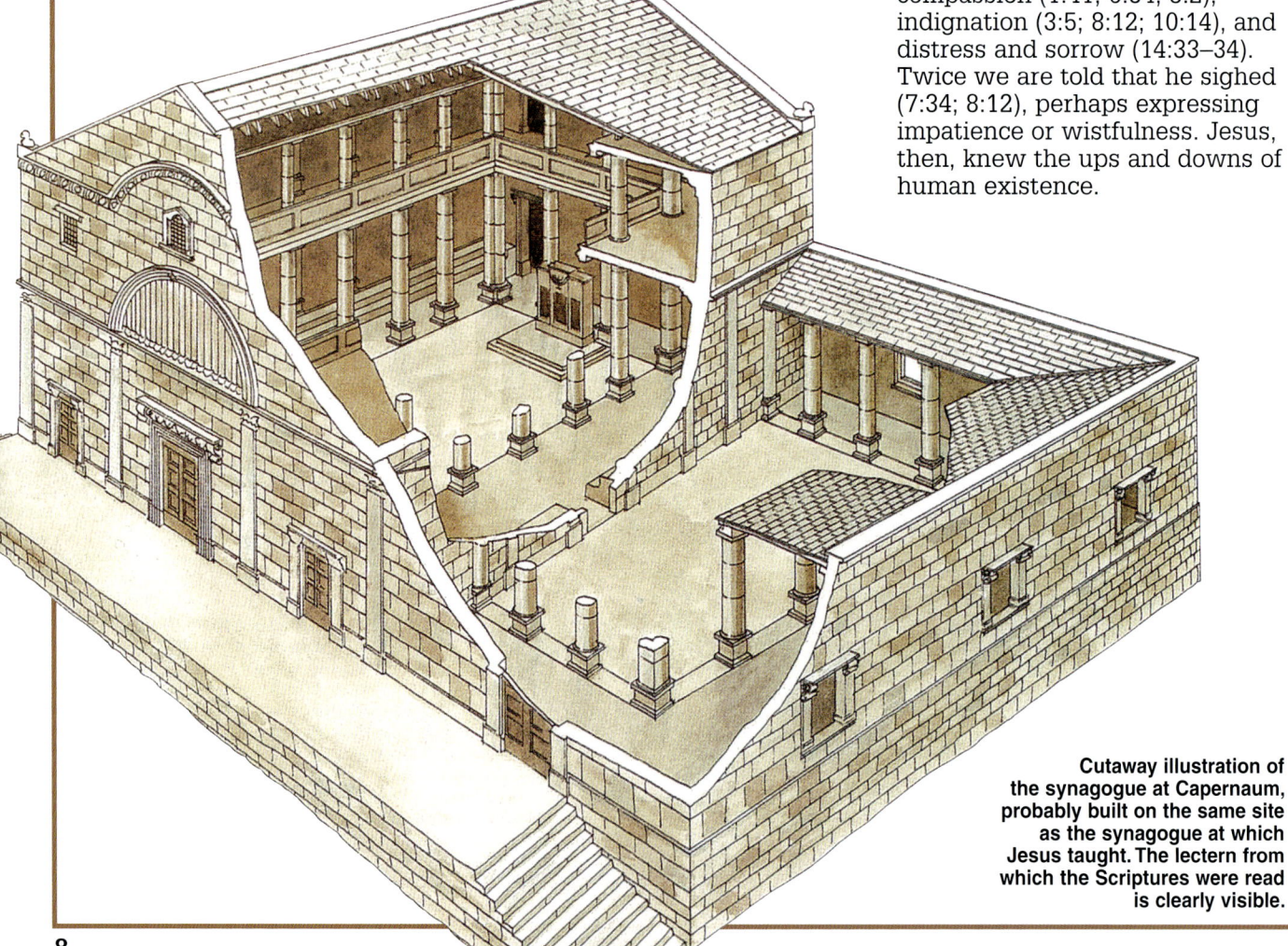

Cutaway illustration of the synagogue at Capernaum, probably built on the same site as the synagogue at which Jesus taught. The lectern from which the Scriptures were read is clearly visible.

A Pharisee at prayer, with prayer shawl and phylacteries.

Yet along with Jesus' undoubted humanity, his divinity, too, comes to the fore in Mark. He is called "Son of God" repeatedly: by Mark (1:1), by the Father (1:11; 9:7), by demons (3:11; 5:7), by Jesus himself (14:62), and by a military officer at Jesus' crucifixion (15:39). Jesus forgives sins, something only God can do (2:7). Jesus is Lord of the Sabbath, one of the pillars of Jewish belief (2:28). He is likewise Lord over nature (4:39), over sickness (6:56), and over death itself (5:42).

An older theory had it that Mark, the first gospel written, presented a mostly human Jesus; then other gospels came along, embellished this picture, and presented a "juiced up" Jesus of divine stature. But this theory is clearly wrong. Mark's gospel may be shorter and more basic in literary structure than other gospels, but the Jesus whom Mark presents is no less God's unique Son sent to save the lost.

Message

What does Mark's gospel communicate overall? Two things stand out.

First, Jesus came to suffer for the sins of others. Long ago a German scholar named Martin Kähler characterized Mark as a passion narrative with a long introduction. "Passion" here refers to Jesus' suffering (Latin *passio*). From 10:32 onward, Mark's gospel focuses on events in Jerusalem and the last week of Jesus' life. Even prior to this, Jesus foretells his death (8:31–38; 9:30–32). That means some 40 percent of the book is devoted to Jesus' last days, ending with the Cross.

Modern preaching sometimes presents Jesus as the secret to human success. If you believe in him, happiness and great blessing will follow. The problem with this teaching is that God grants blessing to both good and evil people (Matt. 5:45). Material blessing is no guarantee of divine favor. The grand goal of Jesus' coming was not to make people affluent. Rather, his coming centered in the cross he endured, by which he won redemption of sinners who would put their personal trust in him.

This leads to the second major aspect of Mark's message: since Jesus the Lord came to give himself for others (10:45), his followers should think of their own purpose in life in similar terms. To be "saved" by Jesus means to lose your own life for the sake of Jesus and the message he proclaimed, which Jesus called "the gospel" (8:34–35). It means becoming Jesus' "disciple," a full-time dedicated student and servant and follower.

Peter, the ultimate human source of Mark's gospel, got it right when he confessed Jesus to be no less than "the Christ," God's chosen ruler and savior (8:29). And Peter was also on target when he described the proper response to Jesus' preaching and call: discipleship. This means, in Peter's words, "We have left everything and followed you" (10:28 ESV).

Outline of Mark

1:1–15	The scene is set
1:16–3:6	Jesus' initial ministry in Galilee
3:7–4:34	Jesus the teacher
4:35–6:6	Jesus the healer
6:7–9:1	On a wider stage: Jesus the Messiah
9:2–10:45	The heart of discipleship: Jesus the leader
10:46–13:37	Jesus the Son of David, the Master of the House
14:1–15:47	Jesus the new covenant sacrifice
16:1–8	The new start

Anyone who wants to follow me must pick up a cross and carry it behind me. If you want to save your life, you will lose it. If you lose your life for my sake and the gospel, you will save it. Mark 8:34–35

Mark 8:34–35

Then he called the crowd to him along with his disciples and said: "If anyone would come after me, he must deny himself and take up his cross and follow me. For whoever wants to save his life will lose it, but whoever loses his life for me and for the gospel will save it." (NIV)

Luke

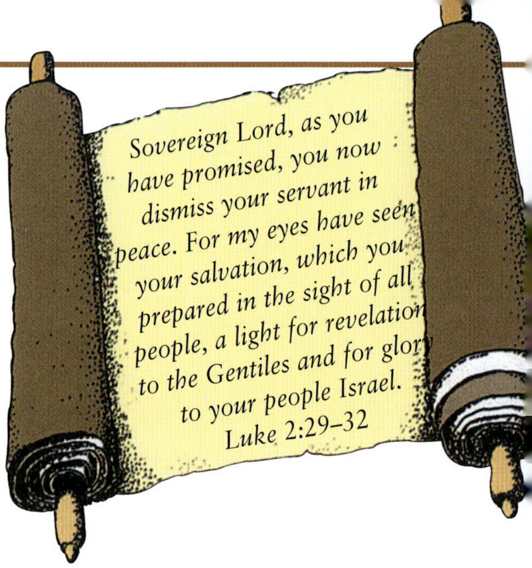

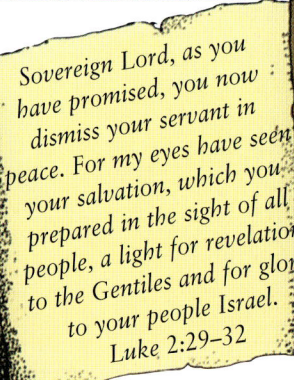

Sovereign Lord, as you have promised, you now dismiss your servant in peace. For my eyes have seen your salvation, which you prepared in the sight of all people, a light for revelation to the Gentiles and for glory to your people Israel.
Luke 2:29–32

The third gospel is really volume one of a two-part work. Volume two is Acts—note how Acts 1:1 speaks of "the first book" Luke wrote. That book was Luke. The outlook and literary style of both writings mark them as coming from the same hand. Luke and Acts together make up more than 25 percent of the New Testament. As a writer, Luke rivals Paul and John for the size and importance of his contribution to the canon.

Who Was Luke?
From his writings it is evident that Luke was educated and intellectually gifted. Based on Acts 1:19 and Colossians 4:14, it seems likely that he was Gentile rather than Jewish. But he certainly understood Jewish matters, in particular the Old Testament Scriptures and their fulfillment in Christ. Luke was a traveling companion of Paul and a medical doctor.

Birth, Childhood and Baptism of Jesus
GALILEE
SEA OF GALILEE
MEDITERRANEAN SEA
Nazareth
Home town of Joseph, Mary and Jesus
Jordan
Scythopolis
4. Joseph, Mary and Jesus return to Nazareth
Salim
Aenon
1. Joseph and Mary go to Bethlehem for Roman census (Luke 2:4)
SAMARIA
Site of John baptizing (John 3:23)
DECAPOLIS
Sebaste (Samaria)
Testing of Jesus for 40 days in the wilderness (Matt. 4:1–11)
5. At age 12, Jesus goes to Jerusalem for Passover Feast (Luke 2:42)
PEREA
3. Jesus is presented in Temple (Luke 2:21)
WILDERNESS OF JUDEA
JUDEA
Jericho
Bethabara
Jerusalem
Probable site of John's baptism of Jesus (Matt. 3:13–17)
Bethlehem
2. Jesus is born (Luke 2:7)
DEAD SEA
IDUMEA
0 25 50 km
0 10 20 30 miles
Journeys of the nativity and childhood
Journey to be baptized

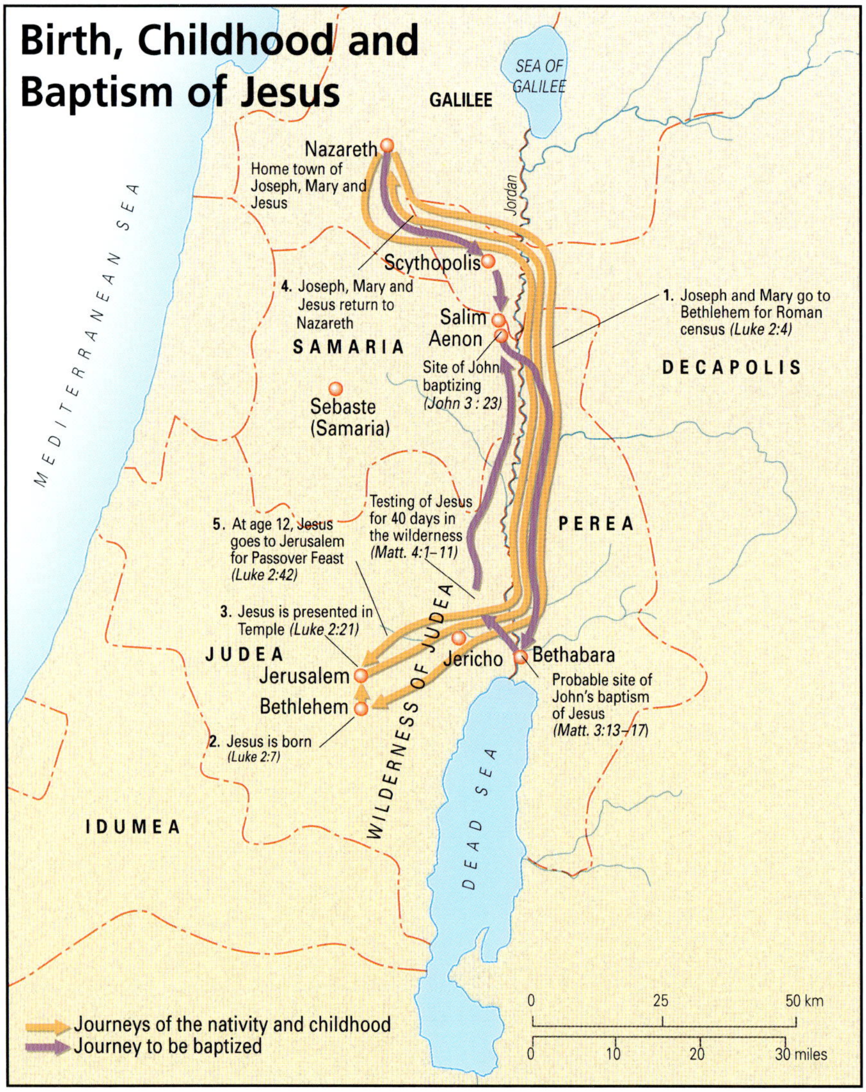

Luke and John
Luke follows much the same outline as Matthew and Mark (except for a very long section, 9:51–19:28, that is largely unique to Luke). But he also has important points of contact with John.

Several people are mentioned by Luke and John alone. These include Mary and Martha, a disciple named Judas who is different from Judas Iscariot, and Annas. Both writers show more interest in Samaria and Jerusalem, and with the temple, than Matthew or Mark. Both speak of Satan's role in Jesus' betrayal (Luke 22:3; John 13:27), of the servant's right ear being cut off (Luke 22:50; John 18:10), of Pilate declaring Jesus innocent three times (Luke 23:4, 14, 22; John 18:38; 19:4, 6), of Joseph's tomb being previously unused (Luke 23:53; John 19:41), and of there being two angels at the tomb on the morning of resurrection day (Luke 24:4; John 20:12).

Was the apostle John one of the "eyewitnesses and ministers of the word" whom Luke interviewed on the way to writing the third gospel?

Luke's Distinctive Outlook

While his overall picture of Jesus fits well with that of the other gospels, Luke reflects unique interest in such matters as

- secular history: no other gospel locates itself so precisely in relation to the larger geo-political scene (see 2:1–2; 3:1–2).
- Jesus' boyhood: most of our knowledge of Jesus' conception, birth, and upbringing are found in Luke 1–2.
- concern for the poor: they are mentioned in Luke as often as in Matthew and Mark combined. Jesus preaches good news to the poor (7:22). Both the shepherds and Jesus' family are poor.
- stress on women: they were often not accorded high respect in first century cultures, but Luke sees women as objects of God's love and key supporters of Jesus' ministry. Such women include Jesus' mother Mary, Elizabeth, Anna, Martha, and her sister Mary, and a group of women who supported Jesus out of their own pockets (8:2–3). Unnamed women also abound: the widow of Nain (7:11–12), the sinner who anointed Jesus' feet (7:37–50), the old woman who was bent over (13:11), the widow who gave God all she had (21:1–4), and the "daughters of Jerusalem" who lamented Jesus' going to the cross (23:28). There are also women in several Lucan parables.
- stress on prayer: Luke highlights Jesus' prayer life (3:21; 5:16; 6:12; 9:18, 28–29; 10:21–22; 11:1; 22:41–42); seven incidents of prayer are found only in Luke. Luke shows Jesus at prayer before each great crisis of his life. Luke alone mentions that Jesus prayed for Peter (22:31–32). Jesus also prays for his enemies (23:34) and for himself (22:41–42). Jesus tells parables on prayer: the friend at midnight (11:5–13), the unjust judge (18:1–8), and the Pharisee and the publican (vv. 10–14). Jesus exhorts his followers to pray (6:28; 11:2; 18:1; 22:40, 46).

Luke the physician, with the tools of his trade.

Outline of Luke

1:1–4	Literary preface
1:5–2:52	The story begins: two wonderful births
3:1–4:13	The turning point in history, the birth of the New Age
4:14–9:50	Jesus' Galilean ministry, in fulfillment of Isaiah 61:1–2 (see 4:18–19)
9:51–19:28	Jesus en route for Jerusalem: the new lifestyle of the Kingdom
19:29–24:53	Arrival at destiny: death and resurrection in Jerusalem

Opening the book, he found the place where it is written, "The Spirit of the Lord is upon me!"
Luke 4:17–18

Summary of Luke's Message

Luke's gospel closes with the unforgettable picture of the risen Jesus telling disciples—twice—that it was the Father's will for the Son to suffer and then be glorified by his resurrection (24:26, 46). These things had been foretold by Old Testament Scripture. Now it is time for his followers to proclaim repentance and forgiveness of sins in Jesus' name (24:47). Later, Acts will describe how this commission began to unfold.

John

Some of the best-loved verses in the Bible are found in John's gospel.

> *In the beginning was the Word, and the Word was with God, and the Word was God.* (1:1 NIV)
> *For God so loved the world that he gave his one and only Son, that whoever believes in him shall not perish but have eternal life.* (3:16 NIV)
> *Jesus answered, "I am the way and the truth and the life. No one comes to the Father except through me."* (14:6 NIV)

These and many other Johannine verses are distinct and memorable. Yet the gospel overall presents the same interpretive challenges as Matthew, Mark, and Luke. John contains a different style and approach, but the Jesus he presents differs little from the one found in the other three gospels.

John the Son of Zebedee

John is prominent in other gospels but is never named in the fourth gospel! Conspicuous by the absence of his given name, he is likely to be "the disciple Jesus loved" mentioned in a few passages (13:23; 19:26; 20:2; 21:7, 20). He witnessed the things he describes (19:35; 21:24), although he obviously cannot report everything Jesus said and did (20:30; 21:25). He was a fisherman from Galilee who responded to John the Baptist's preaching and then moved his allegiance to Jesus when the Baptist singled him out as "God's Lamb who takes away the world's sin" (1:29). He and his brother James were called "the sons of thunder" by Jesus (Mark 3:17), evidently due to their sometimes fiery temperaments (Luke 9:49, 54).

Purpose

John states his purpose: he wants readers to place personal trust in Jesus, "the Christ, the Son of God," so that they will receive the gift of eternal life (20:31). The theme of John is "believing," but believing not by blind faith; another theme of John is "witness" or "testimony." The word often refers to a solemn and sworn declaration of personally apprehended facts. And John's gospel is, basically, a tapestry woven from many "testimonies":

- the witness of John the Baptist (1:19)
- the witness of Jesus (3:11)
- the witness of Jesus' works (5:36)
- the witness of the Father (5:37)
- the witness of the Scriptures (5:39)
- the witness of the Holy Spirit (15:26)
- the witness of the eleven disciples whom Jesus personally chose (15:16, 27)
- the witness of John the apostle himself (19:35; 21:24)

Therefore, while John is sometimes called "the spiritual gospel," it is securely rooted in facts, not just spiritual intuition. John gives compelling reasons for the trust in Christ he calls for.

Titus' Arch, Rome.

A tiled cafe sign in modern Cana. John gives us the wedding at Cana (2:1–11), to which there is no synoptic parallel.

Jesus' Journeys to Jerusalem

Outline of John

1:1–18	The prologue: the Word of God becomes flesh
1:19–2:12	The Word revealed to Israel in the testimony of others
2:13–4:54	The Word revealed as Savior of Israel, Samaria, and the world (Passover)
5:1–6:71	The Word as the Giver of Life (Tabernacles, Passover)
7:1–10:21	The Word and human reaction: faith and dispute (Tabernacles)
10:22–11:54	The Word as the Restorer of Israel (Dedication)
11:55–13:30	The Word prepares for Passover, to lay down his life
13:31–17:26	The Word looks forward to the life of the church
18:1–20:31	The death and resurrection of the Word
21:1–25	The Word commissions the church

These things have been written so that you might believe that Jesus is the Messiah, the Son of God, and so that you might have life through faith in him.
John 20:31

- The Son is every bit as divine as the Father (1:1, 18; 5:18).
- Salvation is rooted not merely in human decision but in God's own personal will (1:12–13).
- Spiritual rebirth is necessary for salvation (3:5).
- To reject Jesus' testimony is to invite God's eternal wrath (3:36).
- Jesus is Lord over sickness and the Sabbath (4:53; 5:16–17).
- Jesus is Lord over death (11:44).
- Jesus gives eternal life to all who trust in him (20:29, 31).

Themes

In addition to "believing" and "witness," John uses a number of other characteristic terms to get his points across. He favors, for instance, imagery involving "light" and "darkness." His doing so in ways similar to usage found in the Old Testament as well as the Dead Sea Scrolls marks John as having more a Jewish background than a Greek one. He loves to speak of "life" and "eternal life." John lays stress on Jesus as "the one and only" Son and "the Son of God." Other gospels more often recall Jesus' use of "Son of Man" to refer to himself, though even John uses the expression about a dozen times. Use of the term illustrates that, overall, much more unites John with the other three gospels than divides his gospel from them.

Teaching

John's gospel contains a wealth of instruction. The gospel makes clear, of course, that salvation is through believing in Jesus' death for one's sins—the Cross—not through flawless obedience to divine instruction. And yet obeying the teaching of John, and of Jesus, is a critical marker of the integrity of faith in Christ. As Jesus puts it, "The person who really loves me is the one who has my commandments and keeps them" (14:21). The following short list of just seven hallowed doctrines found in John must conclude the current too-brief survey of this towering gospel:

Acts

The importance of Acts is twofold. First, it completes what Luke began when he wrote the gospel of Luke. Thus, Acts is the second of a two-volume work. Second, it links the four Gospels with the New Testament letters. It gives some details and many glimpses of how the gospel message went forth across the Roman world in the decades after Jesus died, rose, and ascended.

Luke the Historian
While an ancient "historian" did not operate quite like a modern one, historians of all ages live or die by whether they do justice to the facts they analyze and explain. Luke was not only a literary artist (see previous chapter on Luke); he had mastery of a formidable array of factual data. In Acts he mentions some thirty-two countries, fifty-four cities, and nine Mediterranean islands. The context of these locations is not random, but in the course of a saga lasting some thirty years, extending forth from Jerusalem and rippling out eventually all the way to Rome. He also mentions some ninety-five different persons, sixty-two of whom are not mentioned elsewhere in the New Testament, and twenty-seven of whom are non-believers. Clearly Luke was a writer who did his homework and knew his subject matter.

Purpose
John W. Mauck has recently revived a classic argument that Acts is a legal defense written to be used by Paul when he stood trial in Rome. Mauck's is a plausible hypothesis, but it is one of about a dozen reasons set forth by scholars to explain Luke's intent in writing. These reasons often overlap, and more than one of them is probably valid.

Whatever Luke's personal motivations, Acts begins with a verse (1:8) that is largely agreed to be the book's theme: "When the Holy Spirit comes upon you, you will receive power. Moreover,

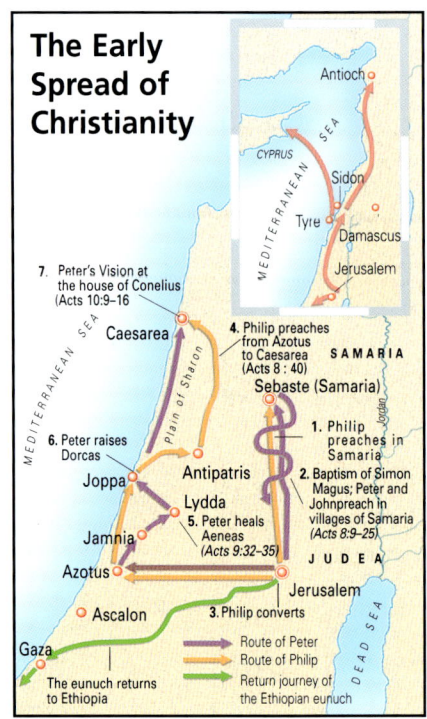

Relief on a Roman gravestone, Philippi, scene of Paul's imprisonment (Acts 17).

you will be my witnesses—in Jerusalem and Judea, in Samaria, and to the ends of the earth." The Book of Acts sketches the spread of the gospel message to these areas through six summary verses:

- 6:7: The word of God spread, and the number of disciples in Jerusalem multiplied.
- 9:31: The church throughout Judea, Galilee, and Samaria was being built up and thriving.
- 12:24: The word of God was growing and multiplying.
- 16:5: The church was growing stronger in its faith and adding members every day.
- 19:20: The word of the Lord was growing and expanding mightily.
- 28:31: Paul preached the kingdom of God and boldly taught about Jesus in Rome.

In the end it seems that Acts completes the purpose for which Luke said he was writing his gospel: to give the reader certainty regarding the grounds of Christian belief (see Luke 1:4)

Luke the Theologian
Part of the genius of Acts is that it combines three elements: literary grace, historical insight, and theological awareness. Acts touches on dozens of Christian doctrines in meaningful ways, three of which are discussed below.

First, Acts emphasizes the work of the Holy Spirit in the salvation of sinners and the rise of the church. From the instruction of the apostles and their empowerment for ministry (1:2, 5, 8), to the coming of the Spirit on the Day of Pentecost (chap. 2), to Paul's application to his listeners of "what the Holy Spirit spoke through Isaiah" (28:25), Acts recounts how God by his Spirit impacts a needy world and in so doing rescues

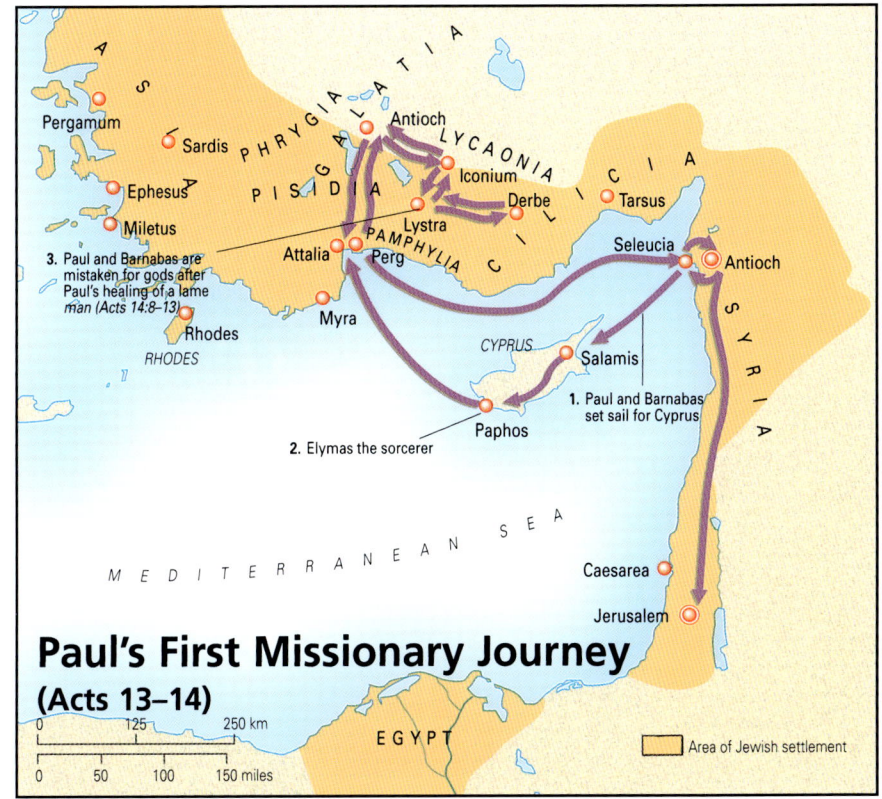

Paul's First Missionary Journey (Acts 13–14)

1. Paul and Barnabas set sail for Cyprus
2. Elymas the sorcerer
3. Paul and Barnabas are mistaken for gods after Paul's healing of a lame man (Acts 14:8–13)

Outline of Acts

1:1–2:47	The story begins: all God's people receive the Spirit
3:1–4:37	The Spirit-filled life: power, boldness, prayer, fellowship
5:1–8:3	Opposition in Jerusalem: the Empire strikes back
8:4–11:18	Victory through defeat: the secret of church growth
11:19–14:28	Bursting out: the Antioch church moves into mission
15:1–35	Fightings within: Jews and Gentiles in the church
15:36–18:22	Paul's second mission from Antioch
18:23–21:16	Off again: from Antioch to Jerusalem via Greece
21:17–26:32	Paul in prison and on trial
27:1–28:31	And so to Rome: the gospel at the heart of the Empire

> You will receive power when the Holy Spirit has come upon you; and you will be my witnesses in Jerusalem, in all Judea and Samaria, and to the ends of the earth.
> Acts 1:8

many from spiritual blindness and destruction.

Second, Acts makes clear that the disciple of Jesus can expect suffering—not every disciple, and not every day, but many disciples much of the time. In Jerusalem apostles are arrested and beaten (5:40); Stephen is martyred (chap. 7); at his conversion, Paul is told how much he will have to suffer for Jesus' name (9:16). Paul applies this suffering to the church in general (14:22), but on a personal level, he realizes that being faithful to Jesus may bring prison and death. Nonetheless, he is ready (21:13). Acts explains how and why this readiness arose—and it still exists today among believers who preserve intact the full force of the apostolic proclamation.

Third, Acts is a powerful reminder that, from the beginning, lying at the core of Christian identity has been mission (a word with a Latin background meaning "sending"). Two massive volumes by Eckhard Schnabel (see "For Further Reading") have recently underscored this point. In the modern West, Acts has drawn attention from scholars as an important historical source. Pentecostal movements have viewed portions of it as a blueprint for their own Christian experience. Contemporary interests should not, however, be allowed to obscure Acts's status as marching orders to all believers to be engaged both in living the gospel and in spreading its benefits into all the world.

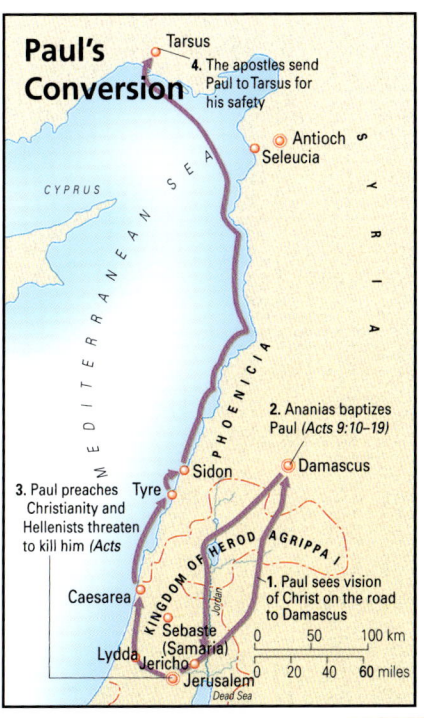

Paul's Conversion

1. Paul sees vision of Christ on the road to Damascus
2. Ananias baptizes Paul (Acts 9:10–19)
3. Paul preaches Christianity and Hellenists threaten to kill him (Acts)
4. The apostles send Paul to Tarsus for his safety

Paul's Early Letters

Galatians; 1–2 Thessalonians

The "Galatian" churches were probably some of the groups founded by Paul and Barnabas in Acts 13–14; the churches of Iconium, Lystra, and Derbe were in or near the Roman administrative district of Galatia. According to Acts, while some received the gospel in these areas, many were angered by Paul's message. Paul was hounded and even stoned and left for dead (Acts 14:19). The time span for these events is around A.D. 48–49. The trip by Paul and Barnabas to plant these churches is called the first missionary journey (see map on page 15).

Gems from Galatians

Paul stood firm against those who misunderstood the gospel message (1:9). God justifies sinners—he declares them "righteous" in his sight—through faith, not by deeds of religious performance (2:16). Old Testament law was designed to point people to their need for God's mercy and ultimately for Christ's sacrifice for their sin (3:24). The Law was not designed to provide moral stair-steps to reach heaven by ethical or religious achievement.

In the course of Paul's animated letter, he makes several memorable statements, commenting that

- even an angel, or Paul himself, should not be heeded if they alter the gospel Paul first preached to them (1:8).
- Christ, in dying for our sins, absorbed in himself the divine curse we deserved (3:13).
- Christ was sent at just the right time in the history of the world (4:4).
- knowing Christ opens up space for the incomparable fruit of the Holy Spirit (5:22–23).
- no human has any ground for moral confidence except on the basis of Christ crucified (6:14).

Galatians may be the earliest letter we have from Paul, but no Pauline letter offers clearer insight into the substance of the saving message of the Cross.

Second Missionary Journey

In the wake of Paul's Galatian letter and further developments, a council was convened in Jerusalem (Acts 15). After the council, Paul and Silas visited churches planted on the first journey. They also pressed on to the city of Thessalonica (Acts 17). There, a church was founded despite so much opposition that Paul and Silas, for their own safety, had to leave at night (17:10). Some weeks after leaving these new believers behind, Paul wrote to them in a letter: 1 Thessalonians. The time of writing was about A.D. 51.

1 Thessalonians

Paul wrote to encourage readers in their newfound faith. Several features of the letter stand out:

1. *Commendation of their persecution.* The Thessalonians had faced fierce opposition (2:14). In the same way Paul was harassed in that city, the Thessalonians "received the word in much affliction" (1:6). But they bore up nobly. One reason for this—Paul warned them it was coming (3:4). This enabled them to stand firm (3:8).

2. *Assurance regarding their future.* Paul's theology was not escapist. Yet he praised readers for living in expectancy of Christ's return (1:10). He spoke of God's "own kingdom and glory," to which the Thessalonians were called (2:12). That kingdom and glory is heaven, and the Lord will return to claim all his people to take them there. Both those who have already died as well

Outlines of Early Letters

Galatians

1:1–10	The single gospel of Christ
1:11–2:21	The single gospel: received, agreed, and defended
3:1–4:31	The single gospel: promised beforehand to Abraham
5:1–6:10	The single gospel: practical consequences
6:11–18	The heart of the single gospel: the cross of Christ

1 Thessalonians

1:1–3:13	Looking back—the gospel in Thessalonica
1:2–10	The people who received it
2:1–12	The apostle who preached it
2:13–16	The enemies who opposed it
2:17–3:10	The messenger who encouraged it
3:11–13	Paul's prayer for them now
4:1–12	In the present—living a holy life
4:13–5:11	Looking ahead—to the coming of the Lord
5:12–28	Living now in the light of the End

2 Thessalonians

1:1–12	The shape of the Christian life
2:1–12	The "rebellion" and the coming of Jesus
2:13–3:5	Belonging to Jesus in the meantime
3:6–18	Business as usual?

We know that a person does not gain acceptance with God by the works of the law, but only through faith in Jesus Christ!
Galatians 2:16

Fact File: Paul

A.D. 34	Converted on the Damascus Road
A.D. 37	First visit to Jerusalem (*Galatians* 1:18; *Acts* 9:26–30). Returns to Tarsus
A.D. 47–48	Ministers in Antioch (*Acts* 11:25–26)
A.D. 48	Second visit to Jerusalem (*Galatians* 2:1–10; *Acts* 11:30)
A.D. 49	First missionary journey—to the Galatian churches (*Acts* 13–14)
A.D. 49	Apostolic Council in Jerusalem (*Acts* 15)
A.D. 50	Writes Galatians. Second missionary journey begins (*Acts* 15:36). Ministers in Thessalonica, arrives in Corinth (*Acts* 18:1)
A.D. 50–51	Writes 1 and 2 Thessalonians

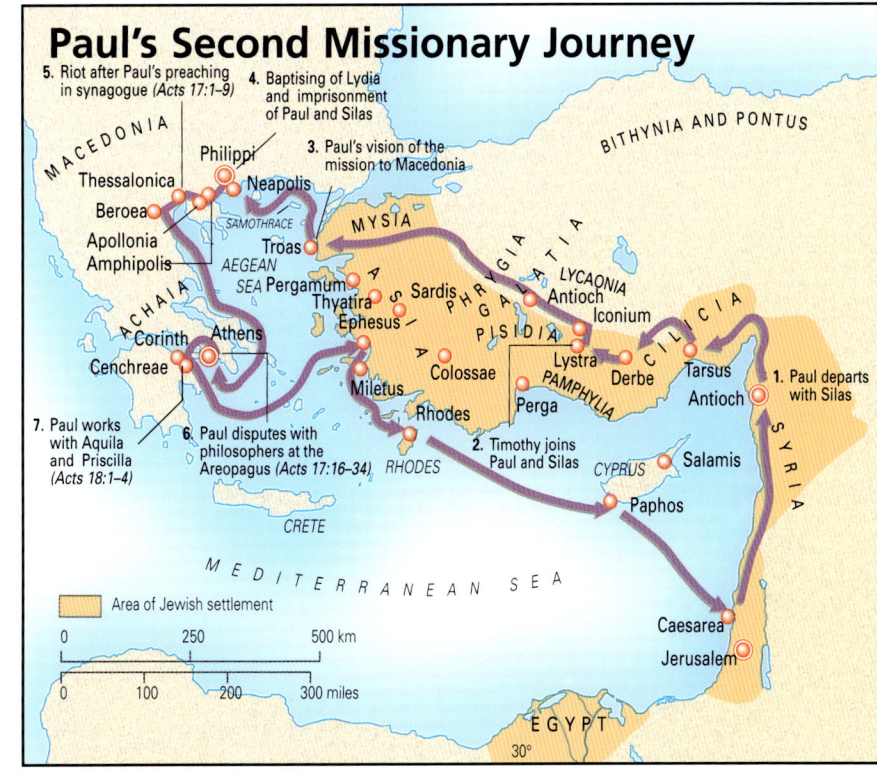

as Christians still alive will be "caught up" to meet Jesus, "and so we will always be with the Lord" (4:17). Paul underscores that the secure future Christians possess because of Christ's return should be grounds in the present for strong encouragement (4:18; 5:11).

3. *The centrality of the Triune God.* When faced with danger, people can turn inward, or even turn on each other. Paul urges the Thessalonians to do neither. He instead focuses their gaze on the Godhead. An illuminating exercise would be to photocopy 1 Thessalonians and, on the copy, underline every reference to God, Jesus, and Holy Spirit.

First Thessalonians bears, then, a profoundly God-centered message.

2 Thessalonians

Not too many weeks after writing 1 Thessalonians, Paul wrote a second letter to them. All three of the themes found in 1 Thessalonians are echoed in this follow-up note. But several matters are singled out for the readers' instruction and strengthening: (1) the judgment to be faced by those who disbelieve the gospel (1:5–12); (2) the gratitude that fills Paul as he remembers the Thessalonians' faith and love (1:3–4; 2:13–15); (3) the need for self-policing in the church. An example of this last matter is that idle busybodies should be corrected and cured of their sloth (3:6–15)! To that end, Paul gives timeless strategies for approaching the problem of lazy church members.

Paul concludes on a note that well summarizes the spirit of all three of Paul's early letters: "Now may the Lord of peace himself give you peace at all times in every way" (3:16 ESV).

Remains of the Roman aqueduct at Antioch, Asia Minor.

Paul and Corinth

1–2 Corinthians

Founding of the Church

Paul wrote his Thessalonian letters (see previous chapter) from the prosperous city of Corinth. He stayed in Corinth eighteen months (Acts 18:11) and, as he wrote, was spearheading the planting of a church there. In doing so, he had help from fellow Jews Aquila and Priscilla, as well as from Silas and Timothy (18:1–5). Later, on his third missionary journey, he wrote 1 Corinthians to them from Ephesus in about A.D. 55.

1 Corinthians: Some Problems

In this epistle it is obvious that the church is facing difficulties. First, the community is rent by factions (1 Cor. 1:10–17). They are spiritually immature (3:1), tolerating flagrant immorality by church members (5:1). Moreover, members are suing each other in civil courts (6:1–8). Subsequent chapters document confusion about marriage (chap. 7), food purchased in the marketplace (which may have been offered as a religious sacrifice in the pagan temples; chaps. 8–10), and behavior in worship (chaps. 11; 14). There was even denial of Christ's resurrection from the dead (chap. 15)!

This congregation seems hardly worth salvaging. But Paul sees hope for them. He doesn't write them off; he exhorts them, "Be vigilant, stand strong in the faith, live courageously, remain steadfast!" (16:13). How can Paul be so optimistic?

Resources for Renewal

Paul knows the gospel has come to the Corinthian church: he preached it to them! And he knows that the message of Jesus creates in hearers faith, hope, and, supremely, love (13:13). These are the fruit of the gospel, which Paul believes can correct his wobbly readers and reconnect them with the truth they first received from Paul, summarized in 15:1–11. But the Corinthians need to come to grips with several things of which they have apparently lost sight.

First, Paul's message has come by revelation, not by human wisdom (2:13). Apparently some were approaching the gospel as a human invention, subject to human disputation and adjustment. Not so, responds Paul. The gospel, like Christ himself, is of divine origin. It is, therefore, to be embraced and not trifled with.

Second, the Corinthians need to pursue unity, not rivalry (3:21–23). This is not a unity that sacrifices truth; it is rather a corporate solidarity growing out of common recognition that the Corinthians' interests and actions are subordinate to Christ and to God. They must stop being ruled by their disparate self-interests.

Third, they must realize that the message of the Cross sanctions morality, not carnality. Paul's own words tell the story here. After quoting a Greek saying, "Bad company corrupts good morals," he urges: "Wake up from your drunken slumber . . . and quit sinning. For some

Remains of the ancient Temple of Apollo, Corinth.

are ignorant of God. I say this to your shame" (15:34). His readers have allowed themselves to be carried along by base and ugly impulses. The gospel, in contrast, produces the urge and means to abound in the work of the Lord (15:58).

Paul concludes by wishing them the full measure of "the grace of the Lord Jesus" as well as Paul's own love for them (16:23–24). A sometimes stern letter has an upbeat conclusion because of Paul's faith in the gospel and his hope for God's people.

A Second Letter

About a year after writing 1 Corinthians, Paul felt compelled to write a letter known to us as 2 Corinthians. He wrote it from Macedonia, well to the north of Corinth, during his third missionary journey. Paul's missionary movements may account for some of the shifts in tone of the letter that careful readers have detected.

2 Corinthians: Important Themes

This letter is intense, personal, and focused. One theme is encouragement. Paul can write, "I rejoice, because I have perfect confidence in you" (7:16 ESV).

Another theme is suffering for Christ's sake. It seems that some leaders there were peddling a message of pain avoidance. Paul knew that faith in the gospel brings the cross of the gospel into believers' lives (4:7–11); Paul's own sufferings are legion (11:23–12:10). There is no other way to follow Christ than to bear up with faith under the difficulties that God's call brings into believers' lives.

A third theme is the sanctity of the apostolic ministry. Paul knows that watered down and distorted versions of the Christian message are circulating. They have even gained a hearing at Corinth, where Paul speaks of "false apostles" in their midst (11:13). Chapters 10–12 are really

Outlines of Corinthians

1 Corinthians

1:1–9	Greetings and thanksgiving
1:10–3:23	The unity of the church around the message of the cross
4:1–21	Paul's self-defense
5:1–6:20	The church and the world: the necessary distance
7:1–40	Christians, sex, and marriage
8:1–11:1	Food sacrificed to idols: willingness to give up one's rights for others
11:2–34	Worshipping rightly in Christ
12:1–14:40	The Body of Christ—one in love and in mutual ministry
15:1–58	The resurrection—Christ's and ours
16:1–24	Wider fellowship: giving to others, greetings from others

2 Corinthians

1:1–11	Paul's sufferings for Christ and for the Corinthians
1:12–2:13	Paul and the Corinthians: pain, forgiveness, and longing
2:14–7:4	Life in Christ: freedom in suffering, the gospel in weakness, hope in the face of death, genuine love
7:5–16	Titus' news and Paul's response
8:1–9:15	Wider fellowship: giving to Paul's collection project
10:1–12:21	Paul, the "super-apostles," and the issue of boasting
13:1–14	Final warnings and greetings

Fact File: Paul

A.D.	
50–52	Ministers in Corinth. Returns to Antioch (*Acts 18:22*)
A.D. 53	Starts third missionary journey. Begins ministry in Ephesus (*Acts 18:23–19:1*)
A.D. 54	Writes 1 Corinthians
A.D. 54–55	"Painful" visit to Corinth (*2 Corinthians 2:1*)
A.D. 55	Leaves Ephesus. "Severe" letter to Corinth (*2 Corinthians 2:4*). Ministers in Troas and Macedonia. Writes 2 Corinthians. Arrives in Corinth for the winter (*Acts 20:3*)

an impassioned defense of the integrity of Paul's gospel labor. Earlier in the epistle, affirming the gospel ministry of reconciliation, Paul makes one of the clearest statements in all of Scripture regarding the meaning of the Cross: "God made him who knew no sin [i.e., Jesus] to be sin on our behalf, so that we might become God's righteousness in him" (5:21). The richness of that statement defies human grasp in full, but at the least it anchors Paul's insistence that the message he preaches goes forth with God's own approval and authority.

Both 1 and 2 Corinthians capture Paul at his best: full of compassion, fervor, wisdom, and God's own love.

Who is weak, and I do not feel weak? Who stumbles into sin, and I do not burn with concern?
2 Corinthians 11:29

Paul and Rome

Fact File: Paul

A.D. 56	Writes to Rome from Corinth. Travels to Jerusalem. Riot, arrest, and hearing before Felix (Acts 20–24)
A.D. 56–58	In prison without trial in Caesarea (Acts 24:27)
A.D. 58	Hearings before Festus and Agrippa (Acts 25–26). Sea journey and shipwreck on Malta (Acts 27:1–28:10)
A.D. 59	Arrives in Rome

At the end of Paul's third missionary journey, in A.D. 56 or 57, he was to be found in Corinth, awaiting a last visit to Rome. It was during this three month stay (Acts 20:3) that he penned a letter to the capital city of the world's most powerful empire: Rome.

Reason for Writing

Scholars have debated why Paul wrote such a long and in some ways complicated treatise. It is obvious that Paul expected to visit the church in Rome soon and from there to undertake a mission to Spain (Rom. 15:24). He needed their prayers (v. 30) and support. But he could have expressed all this with a much shorter note. Moreover, the elaborate opening lines (1:1–6) are without parallel in Paul's other letters. Is there an explanation for these unique features? We can only speculate that for perhaps a number of reasons, Paul felt compelled to dictate to his scribe Tertius (16:22) a full summary of the gospel he preached and some of its implications.

Whatever Paul's purpose, Romans, as a summation and application of a number of key Christian doctrines, has had a powerful effect on church and world history, particularly through the conversion of key individuals who were deeply moved by its message. Augustine was converted as he read 13:12–13; Luther rediscovered the gospel message through reflection on 1:16–17; Karl Barth in the early twentieth century caused a theological revolution in Europe under the inspiration of his study of this epistle.

Practical Counsel (Rom. 12–15)

It is customary to observe that, beginning in chapter 12, Paul focuses on some of the nuts-and-bolts of Christian living. He first exhorts readers to present their bodies a living sacrifice to God (12:1–2). Doing so involves a proper use of spiritual gifts (vv. 3–21) as well as high regard for civic rulers (13:1–7). Christ, not selfish drives and urges, must be Lord (13:8–14), which means cutting slack for the shortcomings of fellow members of Christ's body, the church, so that he, not

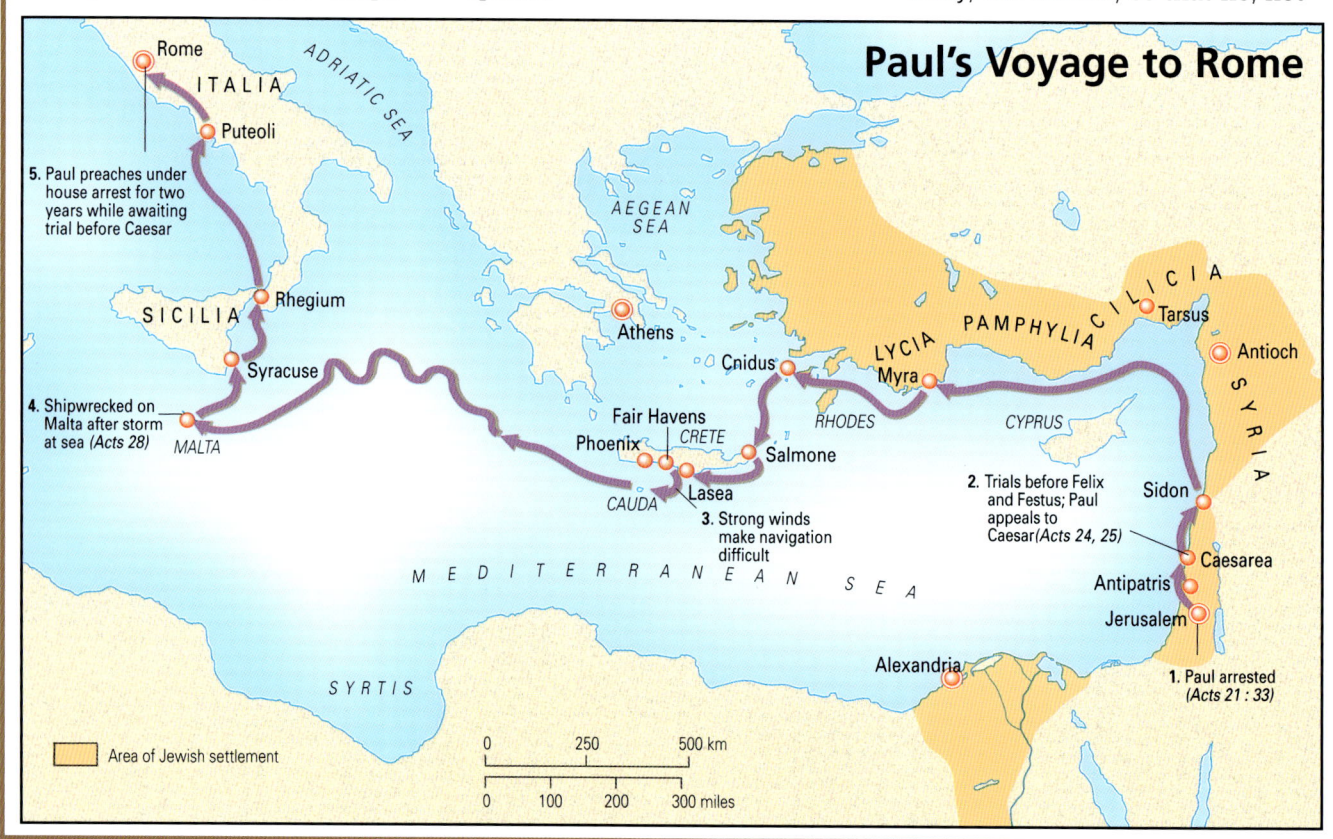

The Forum, ancient Rome.

Outline of Romans	
1:1–17	Paul, set apart to preach the gospel of God
1:18–3:20	The need for the gospel: universal sin
3:21–4:25	The essence of the gospel, illustrated in Abraham
5:1–21	The Man of the gospel: the Christ who dies for us
6:1–8:39	The life of the gospel: death to sin, life in the Spirit
9:1–11:36	The people of the gospel: Jews and Gentiles in God's plan
12:1–15:13	The obedience of the gospel: community in Christ
15:14–33	Paul's ambitions, plans, and fears
16:1–27	Greetings to unite the church

humans, is exalted: "May the God of endurance and encouragement grant you to live in . . . harmony with each other, in line with what Christ Jesus expects" (15:5).

From there, Romans concludes with a summary of Paul's ministry and plans (15:8–32). He also passes along extensive personal greetings (16:1–16) before final admonition and a classic Pauline ascription of praise to God (vv. 17–27). The doxology embedded in this closing section (vv. 25–27) incorporates a telling description of Paul's gospel.

The practical wisdom of chapters 12–15, however, is rooted in the theological bedrock of chapters 1–11.

Bust of the Emperor Nero.

Theological Foundations of "the Gospel"

The most prominent theme in Romans may be found in 1:16–17. There, Paul states programmatically that the "gospel," the "good news" of Christ's death and resurrection, is "God's power that brings salvation to all who believe, because through it God's righteousness is revealed through faith, resulting in faith." Romans, then, from the first to the last chapter, is an explanation of the gospel.

It is impossible to do justice to the richness of Romans in a few paragraphs. Great commentaries, in fact, have been written on Romans by scholars like Cranfield (2 volumes), Wilckens (3 volumes), and Moo (1 volume—but more than 1,000 pages). But this much can be said: in Romans it is taught that

- the "Good News" of God's grace takes shape against the "bad news" of his wrath against sin and ultimately sinners (1:18–3:20).
- God's righteousness is the only remedy for human violation of God's standard, expressed in the law of the Old Testament (3:21–31).
- faith like Abraham exercised is the sole means of laying hold of the promise of the gospel (chap. 4).
- peace with God, shattered through the sin of the first Adam, is restored by justification, which comes through the second Adam, Jesus Christ (chap. 5).
- God's grace in Christ spells the end of sin's reign in believers' daily lives (chap. 6).
- the struggle against sin ends in "no condemnation for those who are in Christ Jesus" (7:1–8:1).
- by the work of God's Spirit, despite Christian suffering in this world, the love of God triumphs (chap. 8).
- the word of God in the gospel has not failed despite Jewish rejection of it, for in the end, God's mercy will, in keeping with God's eternal will, come to Jew and Gentile alike (chaps. 9–11).

The ultimate message of Romans is encapsulated in the wonderment expressed in this flash of insight regarding God (11:36): "For all things are from him and through him and for him—so glory be to him forever. Amen."

Prior chapters have dealt with Paul's earlier and longer letters.

Paul's Later Letters

Prison and Pastoral Epistles

The New Testament contains over a half dozen shorter letters from near the end of Paul's life. Four—Philippians, Ephesians, Colossians, and Philemon, called "the prison epistles"—were probably written during his Roman imprisonment.

It seems likely that Paul was released and did additional traveling and preaching. During this time, he wrote 1 Timothy and Titus. But eventually he was arrested again, which ended for him in a martyr's crown. Shortly before the end he wrote 2 Timothy. These three last letters of Paul are called "the pastoral epistles."

Philippians

Paul wrote this letter to a church he founded (Acts 16:11–40), thanking them for sending him monetary support while he was in jail (Phil. 4:10–20). "Rejoicing" is a prominent theme, a form of that word occurring over a dozen times. Another theme is Christ—he is the very essence of life for the believer (1:21). He is the justification for the suffering to which Christians are called (1:29). He models, and makes possible, the mindset of humility, selflessness, and love for the Father, to which the gospel message beckons God's people (2:5–11).

Ephesians and Colossians

These letters have similar wording in some sections, which may mean Paul wrote them at about the same time. Ephesians has been called "the crown jewel" of Paul's letters for its sublime statements on redemption, grace, atonement, the gospel, and the church. It gives lofty practical counsel on ethics, the Christian family, employers and employees, and the "armor" needed to live as a Christian.

Colossians is slanted a little more toward offsetting false teachers who threaten to hoodwink believers in the town of Colossae (2:8). Paul reaffirms the uniqueness and centrality of Christ (1:15–23) over human religious traditions and mere moral practices (2:16–23). Only Christ renews the soul. Only the saving message about him forms believers who "let the peace of Christ rule" in their midst,

Stone relief of a Roman soldier.

a peace to which they "were called in one body" by the gospel message (3:15).

Philemon

A one-page memo to a slaveholder, Philemon urges mercy toward a runaway slave, Onesimus. It is a model of Paul's love for the lowly, skill in pastoral negotiation, trust in God's Spirit to work in a fellow believer, and humility in persuading rather ordering Philemon to do the right thing. Paul refers all these fine qualities not to himself, of course, but to Christ, mention of whom dominates the letter.

1 Timothy

Timothy had joined Paul on the second missionary journey in the early A.D. 50s (Acts 16:3). Now, a decade later, he is a pastor in the great but godless city of Ephesus (1 Tim. 1:3). Paul urges him to stand firm against all opposition. He uses martial imagery to characterize pastoral labor: sometimes spiritual care is like war (1:18)! Paul gives directions for worship (chap. 2); appointment of pastors and deacons (chap. 3); pastoral morale and duties (chap. 4); care of various groups in the church, particularly widows (chap. 5); and proper regard for money (chap. 6). The letter closes with a stirring appeal for Timothy to "fight the good fight of faith" (6:12).

Remains dating from ancient times of the prison at Philippi.

Remains of the massive theatre at Ephesus, site of the riot caused by Paul's visit.

Fact File: Paul

A.D. 59–61	Under house arrest in Rome (Acts 28:30). Writes Philippians, Ephesians, Colossians, and Philemon
A.D. 61	Charges dropped and Paul released(?)
A.D. 61–64	Ministers again, possibly in Spain (Romans 15:24), Asia Minor (Philemon 22; 2 Timothy 4:13), Crete (Titus 1:5), Corinth (2 Timothy 4:20), Ephesus, and Macedonia (1 Timothy 1:3; 2 Timothy 1:18). Writes 1 Timothy and Titus
A.D. 64–65	Re-arrested, tried, and executed in Rome (2 Timothy 4:6,16). Writes 2 Timothy

Titus

This short letter echoes many themes of 1 Timothy. But Titus oversees ministry in a different region: the island of Crete. Like people everywhere, Cretans have a mean streak (Titus 1:12). Pastoral ministry is no picnic, because humans are ornery. But the gospel can enable people "to renounce godlessness and worldly desires, instead living lives that are self-controlled, upright, and godly" (2:12). Like all of Paul's letters, this one views salvation as a matter of grace, not works (3:5). Yet some half-dozen times, Paul calls Christians to "good works," a reminder that it is not James alone who teaches that faith without works is dead.

2 Timothy

"Come before winter!" (2 Tim. 4:21). It is hard not to see a note of loneliness in Paul's plea to Timothy as he writes. Yet he knows the Lord is near—to him and to Timothy.

Paul recalls Timothy's family background, the glory of the gospel, and the tragedy of believers who fall away (chap. 1). Like a father to a son, Paul commends Timothy to "the grace that is in Christ Jesus" (2:1) as he goes about making disciples and plying the pastoral calling. These last days are full of peril (chap. 3), but the eternal saving wisdom of Scripture stands firm: it is God-given and will uphold Timothy in all he faces (3:14–17).

Timothy should therefore face his life and duties with the same calm hope and fortitude with which Paul eyes his impending death (4:6, 18), pensive but unafraid.

An artist's impression of the Apostle Paul writing from his prison cell.

Hebrews

"The Letter to the Hebrews" makes sense as a title for this book, because it seems to address concerns of "Hebrew" or Jewish Christians. And most of its arguments have direct connection to the Hebrew Scriptures. Modern scholars debate almost every background question about the book: its author, date, place of writing, time of writing, and purpose. But Hebrews was widely accepted in churches from an early date, and the historical questions that cannot be answered precisely with current evidence should not deter readers from an appreciation of the lofty and often original doctrinal formulations it contains.

Christians Under Fire

The book is addressed to readers who made a break with their past religion (probably Judaism) and embraced the Christian faith, despite opposition and persecution (Heb. 10:32–34). But they seem to be having second thoughts and to be drifting (2:1). Now is not the time to throw away their confidence (10:35), for "the apostle and high priest" they confess (3:1), "the founder and perfecter of our faith" (12:2), has suffered for his people. Because of his own suffering, Christ can come to the aid of those who face their own time of trial (3:18).

Masterpiece of Argument

Work by George Guthrie has demonstrated the intricate arrangement of two themes in Hebrews: exposition of various Old Testament passages, and then fervent pastoral exhortation. The writer glides creatively from one to the other, combining deft scriptural interpretation with poignant appeals for faithful response. This rhetorical strategy confirms that the "letter" takes the basic form of a sermon (the meaning of "word of exhortation" in 13:22).

Supremacy of Christ

All interpretation of the Old Testament in Hebrews moves in the same general direction: to demonstrate that Christ fulfills and perfects what the Old Testament began and pointed toward. Christ is superior to the angels (chaps. 1–2), to Moses (3:1–6), to the wilderness rest of God's people under Joshua (3:7–4:13), and to the Old Testament high priest (4:14–5:10). As the sidebar on the next page indicates, Hebrews also contains passages showing *how* Christ perfects the work of both Old Testament priesthoods (Melchizedek's and Aaron's) and even the old covenant itself (see Jer. 31:31–34). Christ not only made complete sacrifice for sin, he *was* the sacrifice (9:12). In addition, the Son, now exalted in heaven, "lives constantly making intercession" for believers (7:25). It is impossible to overstate his excellence and achievement as the dauntless rescuer of otherwise lost men and women.

Dissing the Old Testament?

Since Hebrews shows Christ as the completion of all the Old Testament holds dear, it could be tempting to read Hebrews as rejecting the Old Testament. This would be a mistake. First, logically, all of Hebrews's arguments rest on the sanctity of what God did and what Scripture says about old covenant existence. The argument is not that those things were bad;

Artist's impression of the Jewish High Priest in his full regalia.

The Tabernacle

The author of the book of Hebrews assumes that his readers are well acquainted with the design of the Tabernacle. It was divided into two compartments. The first and larger was the "Holy Place." The further and smaller was the "Most Holy Place," the inner sanctuary. Here stood the ark, surmounted by its golden lid, the mercy seat, where the Shekinah glory, the visible symbol of God's presence, appeared.

The two "Places" were separated by a thick curtain called the veil. By this arrangement the Holy One of Israel was teaching his people both his presence among them, and his inaccessibility to them. He was near and yet far; sinners could draw near, but were not permitted to penetrate into his holy presence beyond the veil. Access to God was limited by four conditions, listed in Hebrews 9:7: *only the High Priest* might enter the inner sanctuary; but *only once a year* (on the Day of Atonement), *and only taking sacrificial blood* with him, to sprinkle on the mercy seat; and then he would secure remission *only for certain sins* (sins "committed in ignorance").

For our author, these limitations showed "that the way into the Most Holy Place had not yet been disclosed" (9:8); once again, the Old Testament reveals its own inadequacy and its need of Jesus. In contrast to the old High Priest, Jesus has "entered the Most Holy Place once for all by his blood, having obtained eternal redemption" (9:12).

Outline of Hebrews

1:1–4	Preface: the Son who is the final Word from God
1:5–2:18	The Son, superior to angels (through whom the law was mediated)
3:1–4:13	The Son, superior to Moses and Joshua (the great old covenant Deliverers)
4:14–5:10	Jesus, the Great High Priest (kernel statement, anticipating [5:11–10:39])
5:11–6:20	1st exhortation to perseverance
7:1–28	The person of Jesus the High Priest (like Melchizedek)
8:1–10:18	The work of Jesus the High Priest (like Aaron)
10:19–39	2nd exhortation to perseverance
11:1–40	Old Testament faith—confidently looking forward, in patient trust
12:1–29	New Testament faith—confidently looking to Jesus, in patient trust
13:1–25	Concluding exhortations and greetings

rather, it is that with Christ a new era has come. Hebrews does not point to an old religion that failed but to a former age in which the fault of God's own people (8:8: "he finds fault with them") paves the way for a fresh covenant having global focus, displacing the older one with its ethnic center in the Jewish people.

Second, Hebrews 11 holds up numerous Old Testament figures as paragons for New Testament believers to admire and imitate. Among them are Abel, Enoch, Noah, Abraham, and Sarah. They exercised the essence of New Testament belief: to look beyond purely this-worldly fulfillment of God's promises to those things that are eternal. They awaited those things that cannot be fully received in this age and this world (11:1, 13, 39). Such is the height of faith in Christ, too (11:40).

Paideia: Assurance of Salvation (Heb. 12:3–11)

Hebrews advances a doctrine that many find startling. Many look for assurance of their salvation in answers to prayer, deliverance from sickness, and freedom from trial and anxiety. Hebrews turns such notions upside down. It views life's adversities, including the world's opposition to Christians, as a sign of God's Fatherhood of his children. To experience *paideia* (Greek word for "discipline," as in a parent "disciplining" a child) is to experience the Father's painful but wise training. Not to thrive on *paideia* is a sign of being a stranger to the God of Jesus Christ, whose grace in "enduring hostility from sinners" (12:3) is presented as a model for believers. Believers are urged to bear the reproach Christ did and not to get too comfortable in this world (13:13), for they have "no lasting city" here, and they live in daily expectancy of "the city that is to come" (13:14). It is immensely helpful that a loving Father works to keep them from getting too comfortable in the wrong ways. True, this does not always feel good to experience (12:11).

1 and 2 Peter

Perhaps the most prominent among Jesus' twelve disciples in the Gospels, Peter is overshadowed by Paul in the Book of Acts. Yet even there Peter is not insignificant, as the missionary work of Paul builds on the foundation God used Peter to establish—from Pentecost, where Peter preached (Acts 2); to the Cornelius incident, where Gentiles were baptized (chaps. 10–11); to the Jerusalem Council, where Peter affirmed the mission of the gospel to Gentile and Jew alike (15:7–11).

These two epistles crystallize the wisdom of Peter in his last years.

1 Peter: Hidden Jewel

This short writing is overlooked by many. Is it because it affirms the blessedness of suffering for Christ, a concept foreign to many in the affluent West? In lands of Christian persecution, 1 Peter is highly regarded. Martin Luther placed it alongside the gospel of John and Romans as the chief "must read" documents for understanding the Bible and the gospel itself.

Peter wrote this epistle to a circle of churches (1:1) from a place he calls "Babylon" (5:13), almost certainly a guarded reference to Rome. The letter assumes a scenario in which some level of hostility to Christians has taken shape in various locales.

Sprinkled with the Blood of Christ (1:2)

In 1 Peter, Christ's "blood" points both to his death for sinners and to the example of suffering to which he calls his followers (4:1). First Peter alternates between references to the blessings that flow from Jesus' unique saving death, on the one hand, and

The theatre, Hierapolis, seat of Papias.

appeals to the fellowship of suffering into which believers are summoned, on the other.

Highlights of Peter's rhetorical strategy include insightful exposition of the Old Testament (chaps. 1–4), stirring recollection of Jesus' example of brave self-renunciation (2:21–25), and frank exhortation to buck up and quit whining when adversity comes calling (4:12–19). In view of the impending end of the age (4:7), Christians are called to humility, sobriety, readiness, resistance, and resilience (5:6–9), for true Christians everywhere face "the same kinds of suffering" (5:9). Despite suffering, however, they can be assured that in due time God will "restore, confirm, strengthen, and establish" them (5:10 ESV).

2 Peter: A Last Testament

Peter's second epistle (3:1) is vague about its place and time of writing. But since the author (named in 1:1) claims to be facing death (1:14), it is reasonable to locate this letter in the mid to late 60s, when Peter is likely to have been martyred.

Second Peter differs from 1 Peter in literary style and vocabulary. But the doctrine of the letter comports completely with what other New Testament writings teach. Highlights of 2 Peter include references to

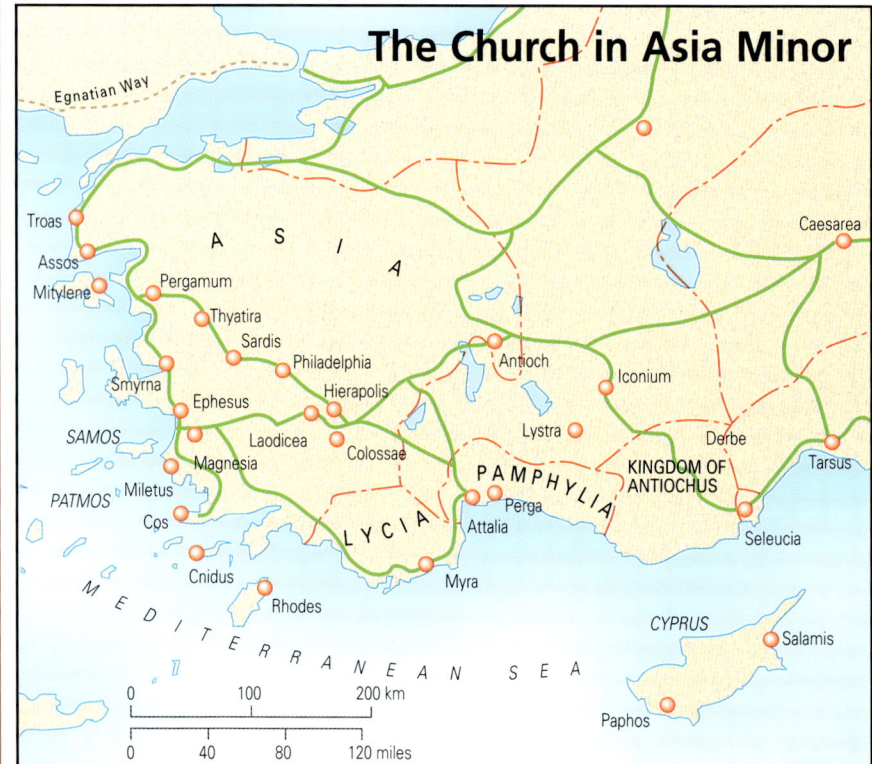

The remains of the Temple of Artemis (Diana) in Ephesus, with (*inset*) statue of Artemis.

Outlines of 1 and 2 Peter

1 Peter

1:1–2:10	**Suffering as a Christian**
1:1–9	The hidden inheritance, the hidden Lord
1:10–2:3	Focus on Jesus
2:4–10	Becoming a Temple, enjoying fellowship with him
2:11–3:12	**Living as aliens in this world**
2:11–12	Keeping your inner self
2:13–3:7	Integrity in difficult relationships
3:8–12	Structuring your corporate self
3:13–4:19	**Suffering— the road to glory**
3:13–22	Suffering for doing good
4:1–11	Living for God
4:12–19	Sharing the sufferings of Christ
5:1–14	**Final exhortations and greetings**

2 Peter

1:1–11	God's call and plan for us: to reproduce his character in us
1:12–2:3	True and false prophecy: holding on to apostolic teaching
2:4–22	Rejecting false teaching and an immoral lifestyle
3:1–18	Living by grace in the light of the End of all things

Jesus' Transfiguration (1:16–18), to the sanctity of Scripture (vv. 19–21), to Christ's return and the end of this age (3:1–13), and to Paul's writings, which are placed on the same level as the Old Testament (v. 16).

False Teaching and Teachers
The emphasis of the letter, like all the New Testament, is on Christ and his completed work. Yet there is frank admission that many people, even in the church, "secretly bring in destructive viewpoints, even denying the Master who bought them" by his death (2:1). Peter, no less than Paul, John, Luke, and other writers, calls God's people to vigilance and calm defense of the truth of the gospel when it comes under attack, as it frequently does.

Assaults on God's will, and rebellion against his reign are as old as the angels who rebelled (2:4). The same apostate impulse saw the light of day in the time of Noah (v. 5), Sodom and Gomorrah (vv. 6–8), and the days of Peter's own readers (2:13–22). Yet "the Lord knows how to rescue the godly from temptation"—and he will also punish those who give in to lawless desires and spurn God's authority (vv. 9–10).

Hope, Not Despair
Despite this grim scenario of unavoidable judgment and destruction of a wicked world, Peter is confident that God does not wish any to perish but desires for all to come to repentance (3:9). So believers should live in obedient expectancy and assurance. Theirs is the priceless privilege, each day to "grow in the grace and knowledge of our Lord and Savior Jesus Christ" (3:18 ESV). Second Peter furnishes rich resources for making this happen.

It is better to suffer for doing good—if God so wills—than for doing evil! For Christ also suffered, once for all, for our sins, the righteous for the unrighteous.
1 Peter 3:17–18

James, John, and Jude

Since the New Testament letters are organized by length, with the shortest coming last, the handful of epistles at the end is quite brief. But none are unimportant. James and Jude were both half-brothers of Jesus; their witness to Christ and the gospel is all the more weighty for that reason. John's stature as a leading apostolic figure grew out of his three years of daily contact with Jesus and was already seen in his authorship of the fourth gospel.

So although these letters are not lengthy, they represent a great storehouse of spiritual counsel and doctrinal substance.

James: "Be Doers, Not Just Listeners!"

Like others in Jesus' family, James was skeptical of his brother during his earthly life (John 7:5). But the risen Christ appeared to him (1 Cor. 15:7), and later he was pastor of the Jerusalem church (Gal. 2:9; Acts 15:13–21; 21:18–25). Early church tradition records that James was martyred in the early A.D. 60s when he was ordered to denounce Jesus as "the Christ" but refused to do so. He left behind a reputation for being a prayer warrior, spending hours daily at the Jerusalem temple on his knees, interceding for fellow Jews who rejected Jesus' lordship.

James's letter has the well-deserved reputation for being practical in orientation. Like the book of Proverbs, James is full of pithy sayings and, like the Old Testament prophets, James is forthright in his calls to repent. It's not enough to "believe" God and the gospel if that just means mental acceptance: the message must be accepted into the heart so that the whole life is transformed.

The theme of James is obedience to the gospel. He lays particular stress on facing trials (chap. 1), impartiality rather than prejudice toward others (chap. 2), speech that is pleasing to God because it expresses divine wisdom (chap. 3), worldliness in its various forms (chap. 4), and the need for prayerful patience (chap. 5). Many themes and words of Jesus are found in James's epistle—including James's repeated call to do God's word, not just listen to it (see Matt. 7:24–27; John 13:17).

John: Truth, Obedience, Love

Historical evidence indicates that late in life John was a pastoral leader around Ephesus. The New Testament contains three letters that have always been ascribed to the same "John" who

Outlines of James, 1 John, and Jude

James

1:1–27	The wise, tested, and reborn life—focused in the three virtues, v. 27
2:1–26	*Virtue 1*: caring for the poor
3:1–4:12	*Virtue 2*: controlling the tongue
4:13–5:6	*Virtue 3*: keeping unspotted from the world
5:7–20	The foundations of the Christian life: patience and prayer

1 John

1:1–2:2	The fundamentals of Christian life and truth
2:3–27	Knowing Jesus in practice
2:28–3:24	Abiding in Jesus in practice
4:1–5:5	Loving God in practice
5:6–21	The secure possession of eternal life through Jesus

Jude

1–4	The need to contend for the faith
5–7	God's hatred of heresy
8–16	What the heretics are really like
17–25	How to respond: remember the faith, live a holy life of love

Ruins of the ancient black basalt synagogue at Chorazin near the Sea of Galilee.

The Death of James

Ananus, who . . . had been appointed to the high priesthood, was rash in his temper and unusually daring. He followed the school of the Sadducees, who are indeed more heartless than any of the other Jews . . . when they sit in judgment. Possessed of such a character, Ananus thought that he had a favorable opportunity because Festus was dead and Albinus was still on the way [that is, there was a vacuum of power between two Roman governors]. And so he convened the judges of the Sanhedrin and brought before them a man named James, the brother of Jesus who was called the Christ, and certain others. He accused them of having transgressed the law and delivered them up to be stoned. Those of the inhabitants of the city who were considered the most fair-minded and who were in strict observance of the law were offended at this. . . .
Josephus *Antiquities* 20:199-201

A coin dating from the Jewish revolt, with the only known depiction of Herod's Temple, Jerusalem. James continued to lead the Jerusalem church in worship there until his death.

Fact File: James

- Jesus' younger brother
- Refuses to "believe" in Jesus during his lifetime (*John 7:5*)
- Comes to faith through a resurrection appearance (*1 Corinthians 15:7*)
- Becomes leader of the Jerusalem church (*Acts 12:17; 15:13*)
- Spoken of by Josephus as a well-known and popular figure in Jerusalem
- Known as "James the Just" according to Hegesippus
- Executed by Ananus the High Priest in A.D. 62 (recorded by Josephus)

---

wrote the fourth gospel. All four writings contain the same style and much similar vocabulary.

Third John addresses an elder named Gaius, a man who showed hospitality to traveling Christian workers (vv. 5–8). Until John can arrive in person (v. 14), he gives Gaius encouragement and some advice for coping with a difficult fellow named Diotrephes (vv. 9–11).

Second John is similar in tone, but it is written to an entire congregation (vv. 1, 13: "elect lady" and "elect sister" seem to describe local churches). John commends them for "walking in the truth" but warns against "deceivers" (vv. 4–11). He will join them soon for a joyous reunion (v. 12).

First John is a powerful statement of a threefold understanding of Christ's coming and message (1:1–4). True believers affirm apostolic doctrine (4:6), obey God's commands (2:3), and are gripped with God's love (4:7). The epistle is a simple-sounding but profoundly nuanced exposition of these themes with exhortation liberally interspersed.

John writes for the sake of the joy he shares with his readers (1:4). John concludes with a warning against idols (5:21). Indeed, in every age there is danger of letting profane objects, ideas, or practices absorb our devotion. John reminds believers that their hearts and hands are Christ's alone to command.

Jude: "Contend for the Faith!"

Jude, a half-brother of Jesus (Matt. 13:55), intended to write a different sort of letter (v. 3). But word must have reached him that his addressees were facing subversive forces. For he ended up writing instead an appeal that his readers uphold the true apostolic faith, even if doing so requires confrontation that is difficult and painful.

Much of the epistle is devoted to profiling the usurpers of Christ's lordship (vv. 4–16). Jude does not mince words: these grumbling troublemakers are nothing more than braggarts and flatterers (v. 16). Some of the rhetoric of Jude echoes themes in 2 Peter.

But in the end, Jude's counsel is constructive. Believers are called to upward growth in faith, prayer, love, and acts of mercy toward those perishing around them (vv. 20–23). All this is possible because God through Jesus Christ is able to keep them from harm and deliver them victorious forever (vv. 24–25). Jude's closing doxology is as rich and moving as any found in the whole Bible.

Revelation

The last book in the New Testament is plainly different from all others. The difference lies chiefly in the kind of writing it is: not a gospel, not a history (like Acts), and not an epistle, but an "apocalypse"—from the Greek word meaning "disclosure." The English word used to render *apocalypse* is "revelation," and that is how the book gets its name. Revelation "reveals" all kinds of things. But it is oriented toward future events, "the things that must soon take place" (1:1).

It should be noted that while Revelation is predominantly "apocalyptic," it can also claim to be "prophetic" and "epistolary"; it is made up of more than one literary type. This make-up adds to the book's richness, but also to the complexity of interpreting it rightly.

Author and Date

In one sense the author is the risen Jesus Christ, as the book's opening words indicate (1:1). Revelation 1:17–3:22 represent Jesus as speaking to John, and here we read Christ's own words. But for the most part, John narrates what he sees. Who is this "John"? The best answer seems to be that he is the apostle who wrote the fourth gospel and the three Johannine letters. Such is the testimony of many early church leaders, and similarities in theology and writing style point in the same direction.

As for date, it can be understood as originating in either the time of Nero (A.D. 60s) or Domitian (A.D. 81–96). Of these two possibilities, the evidence tilts in the direction of the latter. If this is correct, John wrote down these visions very late in life, sometime in the A.D. 90s according to church fathers.

Temple of Trajan, the acropolis, Pergamum.

Remains of the Temple of Artemis, Sardis.

The ancient agora, Smyrna (Izmir).

He was in exile on the island of Patmos at the time (1:9).

Message to (John's) Contemporary Churches

On the whole John has a message for peoples in all times as history moves toward the return of Christ and final judgment. But Revelation has a specific word for seven historic churches found in the region John ministered in and around Ephesus (chaps. 2–3):

- The church in Ephesus has lost its first love and needs to repent.
- The church in Smyrna has faced persecution, and more is on the way. It will receive the crown of life.
- The church at Pergamum had been faithful but is now tolerating false teachers and practices. Repent!

Some of the remaining stone arches of the stadium, ancient Laodicea, Asia Minor.

Outline of Revelation

1:1–20	John's commission, and vision of Christ
2:1–3:22	The letters to the seven churches
4:1–5:14	Christ at the center: the vision of heaven and of a unified universe
6:1–8:5	The seven seals including 7:1–17, the first interlude: the protection of the church
8:6–11:19	The seven trumpets including 10:1–11:14, the second interlude: the preaching of the gospel
12:1–15:4	The seven great portents, explaining God's world
15:5–16:21	The seven bowls of God's wrath
17:1–19:5	The first woman: the fall of Babylon the Great
19:6–22:7	The second woman: the heavenly Jerusalem, the marriage feast of the Lamb
22:8–21	John's commission, and hearing of Christ

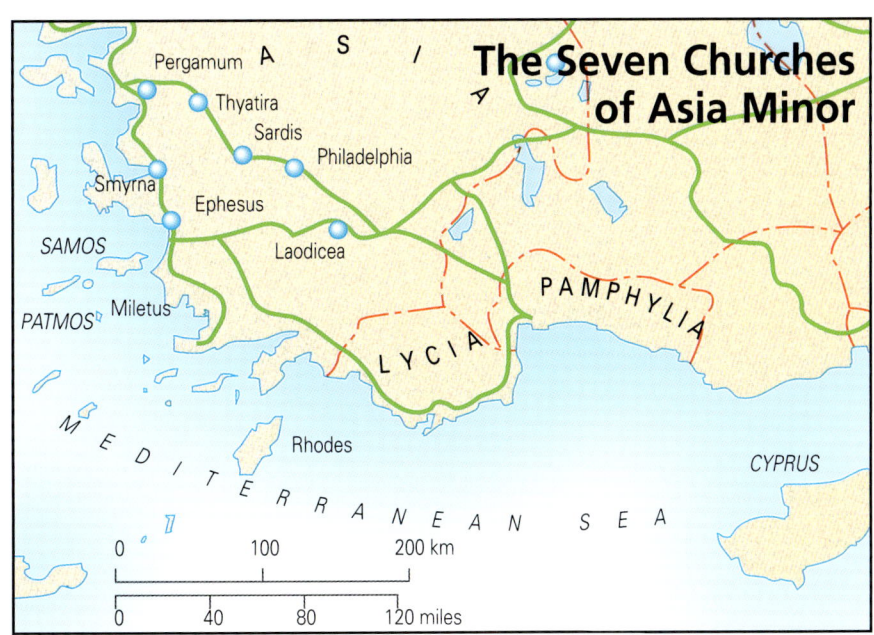

- The church in Thyatira has been rich in works but now gives ear to "Jezebel," who leads the church toward destruction. Some in the church, however, remain steadfast.
- The church in Sardis has a good reputation but is dead in actual works for God. God promises punishment unless they wake up and shape up.
- The church in Philadelphia has kept the Lord's word, and a crown awaits.
- The church in Laodicea is lukewarm but convinces itself that it has no needs. They must "be zealous and repent."

The impression given is that Christ is the hands-on guardian of churches operating in his name. He holds the key to their very survival. Isn't it best to let all things be done in ways that clearly promote his authority and honor? Churches in every age must relearn these lessons.

Images of the End

As the outline in the sidebar indicates, Revelation recounts a series of visions, many of them sevenfold: seven seals, trumpets, signs, plagues, and bowls. It writes of evil's destructive power, but also of God's ultimate triumph. And here it is, in particular, the rider on a white horse (19:11–21) who conquers God's enemies. The rider is God's Son, here called "The Word of God" (v. 13). Satan's final defeat (20:7–10) is followed by the great white throne judgment, where all whose names are not found written in the Lamb's book of life are cast into eternal flames with the Devil, the beast, and the false prophet (vv. 11–15).

This hideous spectacle is offset by a glimpse of the New Heaven and New Earth (21:1–8), the New Jerusalem (vv. 9–27), and the River of Life (22:1–5). Revelation ends with an evangelistic invitation for the reader to come and "take the water of life without price" (v. 17), a reference to personal commitment to Jesus the Lord.

Messages for the Present

Several Christian doctrines find clear expression and extension in Revelation. One is God's sovereignty. He rules over all and will bring all things to the completion he intends. Another is the doctrine of Christ. Again and again he is portrayed in ways really only appropriate to God, as when he calls himself "the Alpha and Omega" (22:13). A third doctrinal emphasis is judgment: eternal blessedness for believers, eternal punishment for the rest, the division lying in individual response to "the lamb that was slain" (5:6, 9), who with God occupies the eternal heavenly throne (22:1). He is coming soon (v. 20), and Revelation urges us all to be ready.

The Library of Celsus, ancient Ephesus.

For Further Reading

Aharoni, Y., Michael Avi-Yonah, and A. F. Rainey. *The Macmillan Bible Atlas.* 3d ed. New York: Macmillan, 2003.

Arnold, C. E. *Zondervan Illustrated Bible Backgrounds Commentary.* 4 vols. Grand Rapids: Zondervan, 2002.

Blomberg, C. *The Historical Reliability of John's Gospel.* Downers Grove: InterVarsity, 2001.

———. *The Historical Reliability of the Gospels.* Leicester: InterVarsity, 1987.

Carson, D. A., and D. J. Moo. *An Introduction to the New Testament.* 2d ed. Grand Rapids: Zondervan, 2005.

Elwell, W. A., and R. Yarbrough. *Encountering the New Testament.* 2d ed. Grand Rapids: Baker, 2005.

Ferguson, E. *Backgrounds of Early Christianity.* 3d ed. Grand Rapids: Eerdmans, 2003.

Finegan, J. *Handbook of Biblical Chronology.* Revised ed. Peabody, Mass.: Hendrickson, 1998.

Green, M. *Thirty Years That Changed the World*: *The Book of Acts for Today.* 2d ed. Grand Rapids: Eerdmans, 2004.

Guthrie, George. *The Structure of Hebrews.* Leiden, The Netherlands: Brill, 1994.

Hill, Charles E. *The Johannine Corpus in the Early Church.* Oxford: Oxford University Press, 2004.

Mauck, J. *Paul on Trial: The Book of Acts as a Defense of Christianity.* Nashville: Thomas Nelson, 2001.

Schnabel, E. *Early Christian Mission.* 2 vols. Downers Grove: InterVarsity, 2004.

Thielman, Frank. *Theology of the New Testament.* Grand Rapids: Zondervan, 2005.

Copyright © 2007 Angus Hudson Ltd/Tim Dowley and Peter Wyart trading as Three's Company

Published in the United States in 2009 by Kregel Publications, a division of Kregel, Inc., P.O. Box 2607, Grand Rapids, Michigan 49501.

All rights reserved. No part of this publication may be reproduced, stored in a retrieval system, or transmitted in any form or by any means—electronic, mechanical, photocopy, recording, or otherwise—without written permission of the publisher, except for brief quotations in printed reviews.

Designed by Peter Wyart, Three's Company

Picture acknowledgments
Photographs
Tim Dowley: pp. 7, 11, 12, 14, 27, 29, 30
Jamie Simson: p. 5
Peter Wyart: pp. 3, 4, 5, 17, 18, 26, 31

Illustrations
Alan Parry: pp. 2, 24
Richard Scott: pp. 10, 23
Paul Wyart: p. 8

Worldwide coedition organized and produced by
Lion Hudson Plc
Wilkinson House
Jordan Hill Road
Oxford OX2 8DR
Tel: +44 1865 302750
Fax: +44 1865 302757

ISBN 978-0-8254-4170-7

Printed in China

Unless otherwise indicated, all Scripture quotations are the author's translation.

Scripture quotations marked ESV are taken from The Holy Bible, English Standard Version, copyright © 2001 by Crossway Bibles, a division of Good News Publishers. Used by permission. All rights reserved.

Scripture quotations marked NIV are taken from the *Holy Bible, New International Version*®.
Copyright © 1973, 1978, 1984 by International Bible Society. Used by permission of Zondervan. All rights reserved.